Silent Depths

A Cold War Submarine Thriller

By Art Venka

Silent Depths: A Cold War Submarine Thriller
By Art Venka

Dive into the heart-pounding depths of the Cold War with *Silent Depths*, a gripping tale of espionage, survival, and sacrifice beneath the waves. Combining the intensity of modern submarine fiction with the intrigue of Cold War espionage history, this novel takes you on a harrowing journey through the shadowy world of naval warfare.

The USS Oregon, an advanced American submarine, is tasked with a top-secret mission to infiltrate Soviet waters and uncover classified intelligence. As the crew navigates the icy depths of the Barents Sea, they face relentless Soviet patrols, technical malfunctions, and the chilling realization that danger may lurk not just outside their vessel, but within.

Told with unflinching realism and packed with suspense, *Silent Depths* weaves a narrative of tactical brilliance and human endurance. From the claustrophobic tension of the submarine's control room to the vast, hostile ocean, every page immerses readers in a high-stakes battle of wits and survival.

For fans of **books about submarines**, **Cold War fiction books**, and **thriller novels about war**, this story captures the essence of naval warfare, the sacrifices of its crew, and the moral complexities of espionage. Whether you're drawn to **naval war books**, **war story novels**, or tales of unyielding courage, *Silent Depths* promises to keep you on the edge of your seat.

- **Espionage History Books:** Explore the covert operations that defined the Cold War.
- **Naval Books and Submarine Fiction:** Experience the pulse-pounding drama of life below the waves.
- **Men Stories:** Witness the bonds, conflicts, and resilience of those who serve.
- **Books About Naval Battles:** Engage in thrilling underwater conflicts and strategic maneuvering.

Prepare for an unforgettable journey into the silent, shadowed depths of Cold War history.

Part 1: Departure into the Unknown

The Atlantic stretched endlessly, its surface a restless expanse of dark, churning waves. Beneath the steel-gray sky, the USS *Oregon* loomed in the shadows of the naval dock. The submarine's sleek, black hull glistened faintly under the harsh glare of the floodlights, an imposing silhouette poised for its plunge into the unseen depths. The atmosphere was thick with anticipation, the kind that hung heavy in the air before the unknown swallowed the familiar.

Around the dock, the last remnants of the pre-departure hustle played out—crews securing hatches, final checks being called out over crackling radios, the clatter of boots on steel. Yet, within the submarine itself, there was a profound stillness, broken only by the muted hum of machinery. The *Oregon* was alive, its systems primed, its purpose clear.

In the control room, Captain Robert "Bob" King stood tall, a figure of quiet command amidst the controlled chaos. His hands were clasped behind his back, the tailored lines of his uniform emphasizing the unyielding precision of his stance. He was the axis around which the room revolved, his mere presence a steadying force.

King's piercing gaze swept over his crew, each member immersed in their duties. There was no room for doubt here, though he could sense the undercurrent of tension—a collective unease buried beneath their disciplined exteriors. This was no ordinary deployment. The mission ahead was one of shadows and silence, where mistakes carried the weight of international conflict.

"Mr. Landry," King's voice cut through the room with calm authority, drawing the attention of the boatswain.

Joe Landry, a seasoned veteran with a weathered face that told stories of decades at sea, turned from his station. His gruff demeanor was matched by an unshakeable competence, the kind earned through years of service in unforgiving waters.

"All systems green, sir," Landry reported, his voice steady. "Crew secured, and we're ready for submersion."

King nodded, the briefest acknowledgment before his attention shifted to the map spread across the navigation table. The *Oregon's* route was carefully charted, a winding path that would lead them north through the Atlantic, skimming the icy edges of the Arctic Circle, and into the Barents Sea. It was a journey fraught with danger, a clandestine mission that would bring them perilously close to Soviet territory.

"Helm," King ordered without turning, his gaze fixed on the map. "Prepare for submersion. Take us to operational depth, heading zero-two-five degrees."

"Yes, sir," came the prompt response, followed by the low whine of the ballast tanks as the submarine began its descent.

The crew moved with practiced efficiency, their hands flying over consoles and switches with precision honed by countless drills. The dim lighting of the control room added to the sense of isolation, the outside world already fading as the *Oregon* slipped beneath the surface.

Nearby, Lieutenant Emily Carter monitored the sonar station, her eyes darting between screens with razor-sharp focus. A quiet intensity defined her, the weight of her role clear in the set of her jaw. She was the crew's eyes and ears in the black void of the deep, and her dedication was matched only by her resolve to prove herself in an environment where doubt could mean disaster.

"All stations, report readiness," King commanded, his tone calm but firm.

One by one, the confirmations came in—a chorus of voices blending into a symphony of discipline. Each word carried a note of certainty, but beneath the surface lay the unspoken acknowledgment of the stakes.

As the *Oregon* settled into its operational depth, the outside world disappeared completely, replaced by the low hum of machinery and the occasional groan of the hull under pressure. Inside, the crew settled into the rhythm of the mission, their movements purposeful and precise.

King allowed himself a moment to study the faces around him—Landry's quiet resolve, Carter's unwavering focus, Green's steady confidence at the navigation console. These were the people he would trust his life with in the days ahead, the ones who would carry this mission on their shoulders alongside him.

"Mark the log," he said finally, his voice steady. "Mission begins at oh-eight-hundred hours."

There was no room for hesitation now. The *Oregon* was committed, its course set, its crew united under a single purpose. As the submarine glided deeper into the Atlantic, its presence became a phantom in the depths—a vessel of silence, moving steadily toward the unknown.

Part 2: Internal Tension

The narrow corridors of the *Oregon* buzzed with muted activity, every sound amplified by the submarine's confined steel walls. The clang of boots on the gridded floor reverberated like distant echoes, while orders were exchanged in low, clipped tones. The usual camaraderie of the crew was absent, replaced by a collective focus that bordered on palpable tension.

The scent of oil and machinery mingled with the faint tang of saltwater, creating an atmosphere unique to life beneath the waves. Sailors moved purposefully, their expressions guarded, their movements sharp. Every task carried the weight of the mission, and every shadow in the dim lighting seemed to whisper of the dangers awaiting them.

In the navigation bay, Lieutenant Thomas Green hunched over his station, his brow furrowed in deep concentration. The glow of the control panel cast a pale light across his face as his fingers moved with practiced precision, recalculating their course for the tenth time in as many hours. Despite his outward composure, the enormity of the mission gnawed at his nerves, a constant undercurrent beneath his determination.

The young officer paused briefly, his eyes scanning the map. It was a route laced with peril, threading through uncharted currents and avoiding commercial lanes and known patrol zones. He exhaled slowly, his breath fogging the glass of the display for a moment before he wiped it clean with a sleeve.

"How's it looking, Tom?" Joe Landry's voice broke the silence, its familiar gruffness a grounding force. The seasoned boatswain leaned against the bulkhead, his arms crossed over his chest, his presence as steady as the submarine itself.

Green straightened slightly, though his grip on the edge of the console betrayed his lingering unease. "Solid," he replied, his voice steady but tinged with the weight of responsibility. "We'll stick to the thermocline and stay below the shipping lanes. If we hold this depth, they won't see us coming."

Landry grunted in approval, his weathered face creasing into a rare, faint smile. "Just keep us steady, kid," he said, clapping Green on the back with a force that nearly unbalanced him. "The captain's counting on you, and so are the rest of us."

A few feet away, Lieutenant Emily Carter sat at her station, her posture a study in unyielding focus. The flickering green glow of incoming sonar data reflected in her sharp eyes as she sifted through endless streams of information. She was a singular presence aboard *Oregon*, her role as the only woman on the submarine placing her under constant scrutiny. But skepticism had long been silenced by her unwavering precision and razor-sharp analytical mind.

Her fingers moved deftly over the keys, isolating weak signals and filtering out the ambient noise of the ocean. She hardly noticed the whispered conversations that floated through the room, fragments of unease threading their way into the air like an invisible mist.

"You think they know we're coming?" a young sailor murmured to his companion, his voice barely audible over the hum of the equipment.

"If they do," came the grim reply, "we'll never see it coming."

Carter's head snapped up, her expression cutting through the air like a blade. Her voice was low but firm, each word laced with authority.

"Focus on your tasks, not speculation," she said curtly, silencing the pair. The tension was thick enough without idle fear eroding their resolve.

Across the control room, the captain's presence lingered like an anchor. Though King's words were few, his watchful gaze was ever-present, a steady reminder of the stakes they faced. His confidence radiated outward, a force that steadied the crew even as the specter of uncertainty loomed large.

For now, the *Oregon* moved in near-silence through the depths, the pulse of her engines a low, constant thrum. Each creak of the hull under pressure seemed louder in the silence, each whisper of water against the steel a reminder of the invisible dangers surrounding them.

And yet, within the submarine, every individual worked in harmony, their efforts coalescing into a singular purpose. Beneath the tension, there was a quiet understanding: they were a team, bound by their mission and their trust in one another.

The stakes were high, and the challenges lay ahead like an unbroken wave. But for now, they pressed forward, their resolve as unyielding as the ocean itself.

Part 3: Submersion and Departure

"Dive stations!" The command cut through the air like a sharp blade, precise and authoritative. Captain King's voice, steady yet commanding, echoed through the *Oregon*, igniting a flurry of controlled activity. Crew members moved with practiced efficiency, sealing hatches, checking gauges, and securing stations. The submarine hummed to life, her engines vibrating faintly through the steel hull, a deep, resonant growl that signaled her readiness to embrace the depths.

The *Oregon* began its slow descent, slipping beneath the surface of the Atlantic with the grace of a predator. Water cascaded over her hull, swallowing her whole until she vanished into the cold, shadowy embrace of the ocean. The surface, turbulent moments ago, stilled as though erasing all evidence of her existence.

In the control room, the lighting dimmed to a subdued glow, casting long shadows across the faces of the crew. The flickering green and amber displays created an eerie, otherworldly atmosphere, a stark contrast to the chaos of the dock mere hours ago. Captain King stood tall at the center, his hands lightly clasped behind his back, a pillar of focus amidst the subdued hum of activity around him.

"Helmsman," he said, his tone unyielding, "take us to 200 feet. Maintain course zero-five-zero."

"Aye, sir," the helmsman replied, his hands steady on the controls.

The submarine's descent was almost imperceptible to those within, but the creak of the hull under pressure spoke volumes about the forces at play outside. Each groan of steel was a subtle reminder of the ocean's immense power, a force that would crush them without hesitation if they strayed too deep or too far from their limits.

At the sonar station, Lieutenant Carter monitored the hydrophone feed, her sharp eyes scanning the readings with unwavering focus. Her ears were attuned to the subtle symphony of underwater sounds—the faint whisper of distant currents, the soft echo of marine life, and the rhythmic thrum of *Oregon's* own engines.

"We're clear of the surface," she reported, her voice calm and precise. "No active contacts detected."

King nodded, his gaze fixed ahead. "Good. Keep monitoring. I want updates every ten minutes. We can't afford any surprises."

Carter's fingers danced over the console as she refined the sonar filters, isolating potential signals from the ambient noise. The crew around her worked in practiced silence, the occasional exchange of clipped orders punctuating the steady hum of the vessel's systems.

The submarine glided deeper, the ocean outside transitioning from a dull, murky blue to a pitch-black void. The world above disappeared entirely, replaced by the infinite pressure of the depths. Inside the *Oregon*, the crew settled into their roles with a precision born of rigorous training.

But beneath the polished façade of routine, an unspoken tension lingered—a silent specter that haunted every corner of the vessel.

For each member of the crew, the mission was a test of endurance, not just of their skills but of their nerves. Every movement, every decision carried the weight of their objective: to penetrate unseen into hostile waters and gather intelligence vital to their nation's security. There was no room for error, no margin for failure.

As the *Oregon* leveled off at 200 feet, the hull creaked softly in protest against the mounting pressure. The sound was familiar but no less unsettling, a subtle reminder of their fragile existence in a world designed to destroy them. Yet, within the submarine, there was no fear—only focus.

King's eyes moved across the control room, taking in the faces of his crew. Each expression was a study in concentration: Carter's sharp focus on the sonar feed, Green's calculated adjustments at the navigation console, Landry's quiet vigilance at his post. This was his team, his responsibility, and in their competence, he found reassurance.

"Mark this position," King ordered, his voice steady. "The mission begins here."

The submarine continued its silent journey, slipping further into the abyss. The *Oregon* was now a ghost, unseen and unheard, moving with purpose through the dark, unforgiving depths of the Atlantic. The surface world was far behind them, and ahead lay the unknown—both their mission and the dangers that would seek to end it.

For now, the ocean held its breath, and so did they.

Part 4: Into Hostile Waters

Two days of endless ocean had passed, the Barents Sea now stretching before the *Oregon* like an icy gauntlet. The Atlantic's familiar rhythm had given way to a more foreboding tone—quieter, darker, as if the sea itself recognized the danger ahead. The submarine pressed forward, its sleek hull cutting silently through the frigid depths, carrying its crew into the heart of enemy territory.

Inside, the atmosphere had shifted. The tension that once simmered beneath the surface now clung to every corner of the vessel. Each creak of the hull and hum of machinery felt amplified, a subtle reminder of the dangers that surrounded them. This was Soviet territory—every mile bristled with patrols, sensors, and the ever-present threat of detection. Here, discovery would mean not just failure, but annihilation.

In the dimly lit mess hall, sailors gathered in uneasy clusters, their voices low, their conversations oscillating between nervous humor and the grim reality of their mission. Plates sat half-finished on the tables, more a display of habit than appetite. The air smelled faintly of reheated coffee and the metallic tang of recycled air—a constant reminder of their isolation beneath the waves.

Lieutenant Green sat alone in the corner, his tray untouched. His gaze was fixed on the table, his fingers drumming an uneven rhythm. The burden of his responsibilities weighed heavily on him. Every course correction, every calculation—each one felt like a thread in the thin line between survival and disaster.

Across the room, Carter was hunched over her notebook, the glow of a nearby panel casting sharp shadows across her features. Her pencil moved rapidly across the page, sketching out contingencies, alternate routes, and scenarios for every possible emergency. Her mind raced with probabilities, her determination unwavering. If the mission demanded precision, she would provide it.

The low hum of the intercom broke through the quiet, crackling for a moment before Captain King's voice came through, calm but commanding.

"Attention, all hands. Prepare for silent running."

The mess hall fell into an immediate, profound silence. The sailors exchanged brief glances before moving purposefully to their stations. The weight of those words was not lost on them. Silent running was more than a protocol—it was a transformation.

Silent running meant reducing the *Oregon* to a ghost, an invisible presence in the abyss. All nonessential systems would be powered down. Lights dimmed, engines hushed to a whisper. Every movement, every sound had to be calculated, deliberate. Even a dropped wrench could echo through the water and betray their position to enemy hydrophones.

As the crew settled into their posts, King's voice returned, this time with an edge of steel.

"This mission demands the best from all of us," he said, each word measured, deliberate. "Stay sharp. Stay focused. Remember—every decision we make out here matters."

His words reverberated through the submarine, settling over the crew like a shared mantra. Each sailor carried their own fears, but together they formed a collective resolve. They were not individuals—they were *Oregon*, a single entity moving toward a singular goal.

The submarine pressed forward, the water around it growing colder, heavier. At the sonar station, Carter adjusted her filters, listening for the faintest traces of enemy activity. Green monitored the navigation panel, his eyes scanning for hidden dangers in the shifting currents. Landry paced quietly, his practiced movements steady as he double-checked critical systems.

The *Oregon* crossed the invisible boundary into Soviet waters, the tension in the control room thick enough to touch. The crew's breathing was slow and measured, their focus razor-sharp. For a moment, there was only the hum of the vessel and the muted groan of the ocean's embrace.

But beneath the quiet, the stakes loomed large. Every mile deeper into enemy territory was a step further from safety. The Barents Sea was not just a place—it was a crucible, one that would test their skill, their discipline, and their will to survive.

King stood at the helm, his hands resting lightly on the edge of the console. His gaze was steady, unflinching. The weight of command bore down on him, but he welcomed it. This was what he was trained for, what they all were trained for.

As the *Oregon* slipped deeper into the hostile waters, the world above seemed to fade into memory. The submarine was no longer a part of that world; it was a shadow, moving with purpose and precision, invisible yet determined.

The mission had truly begun, but the dangers that lay ahead loomed like storm clouds on the horizon, waiting for the right moment to strike.

Part 5: First Signs of the Hunt

The *Oregon* slipped deeper into Soviet waters, its steel hull a silent sentinel against the encroaching darkness. Every meter carried them closer to danger, and the submarine itself seemed to absorb the weight of the crew's unspoken fears. Conversations had dwindled to near silence, and even the rhythm of footsteps on the grated floors was softer, as though every sound risked betraying their presence.

The pressure of the ocean was a constant companion, its immense force groaning against the submarine's frame. To the crew, each creak was amplified in the stillness, a visceral reminder of the fragility of their vessel. The air inside felt heavier, laden with tension and the knowledge that they were now within the lion's den.

In the sonar room, the atmosphere was especially thick. The dim lighting illuminated Petty Officer Daniels as he sat hunched over his station, his headphones clamped tightly to his ears. A low hum filled the room, the rhythmic pulse of the sonar monitor punctuated by faint pings from the vastness of the ocean. His hands hovered over the controls, adjusting dials with the precision of a surgeon.

Then, a sound—a persistent, calculated ping—cut through the feed. Daniels froze for a moment, his breath caught in his throat. The noise was distant but deliberate, a telltale signature of an active sonar sweep. His fingers flew over the console, isolating the signal, sharpening its clarity until its source became unmistakable.

"Lieutenant Carter," Daniels called softly, his voice barely louder than a whisper, as though afraid the sound might carry through the steel walls. "You'll want to hear this."

Emily Carter, already attuned to the room's shift in tension, was at his side in an instant. She leaned over his station, her sharp gaze scanning the screen before reaching for a pair of headphones. Sliding them on, she closed her eyes for a brief moment, focusing entirely on the sound.

There it was—faint but deliberate, a Soviet patrol vessel combing the depths with its sonar. Each ping reverberated through the hydrophone, an auditory spotlight sweeping the ocean for intruders.

"It's six, maybe six and a half kilometers out," she said, her voice calm but edged with focus. "They're scanning, but... they don't know we're here. Yet."

Her words hung in the air like a taut wire, the weight of "yet" pulling at every ear in the room.

Moments later, Captain King entered, his presence as commanding as ever. He had been summoned not by a direct call but by the subtle shift in the crew's demeanor—an unspoken signal that something had changed. His sharp eyes darted to the monitor as Carter briefed him, her words concise but comprehensive.

King's jaw tightened slightly, a fleeting crack in his otherwise impenetrable composure. He listened to the faint pings through the headphones Daniels handed him, his mind already calculating the next move.

"Helmsman," he said, his voice steady, each syllable carrying the weight of command, "reduce speed to one-third. Maintain depth. Let's stay in the thermocline and keep our profile minimal. We'll let them think these waters are empty."

The order rippled through the crew like an electric current. The helmsman adjusted the controls, the hum of the engines dropping to a near-whisper. The *Oregon* slowed its glide, becoming a shadow among shadows, blending into the cold, icy depths.

The crew moved with practiced precision, their movements calculated, deliberate. In the sonar room, Carter and Daniels remained glued to their monitors, their ears attuned to every subtle shift in the signal. The faint pings persisted, their rhythm steady and searching.

King stood near the center console, his hands lightly resting on its edges, his mind racing through possibilities. The *Oregon* had the advantage of stealth, but the Soviet patrol vessel wasn't simply patrolling—it was hunting.

"We're ghosts," King murmured softly, almost to himself. "And ghosts leave no trace."

The *Oregon* pressed forward, its journey a delicate dance between precision and peril. Outside, the ocean was a void, vast and indifferent, while inside, the crew worked in synchrony, each individual a vital cog in the machine of survival.

The faint pings began to fade, but no one relaxed. It wasn't relief—it was merely the calm before the storm, the pause before the enemy's next move.

For now, they remained unseen, a phantom in the depths. But the hunt had only just begun.

Part 6: Shadows in the Depths

The patrol vessel's sonar pings faded into the distant murmur of the ocean, growing more sporadic as the Soviet ship shifted its search pattern. Still, no one aboard the *Oregon* relaxed. The silence in the control room was suffocating, heavy with unspoken fears and the oppressive weight of the water pressing down on them. The faint hum of the submarine's systems was the only sound, a subtle reminder of their precarious existence in the abyss.

Captain King stood at the helm, his posture rigid but his face calm—a mask of confidence he wore for his crew. He pressed the intercom button, his voice breaking the stillness like the crack of a whip.

"Good work, everyone. But this is just the beginning. Stay sharp, stay focused."

The words were measured, intended to instill reassurance, but they carried an undeniable gravity. Everyone aboard knew the truth: the patrol vessel they had evaded was merely the first in what would undoubtedly be a series of challenges. Their mission demanded not just stealth but relentless precision and unwavering endurance. The ocean was vast, but danger was closer than it appeared.

Below deck, the tension was no less palpable. In the navigation bay, Thomas Green sat hunched over his console, his fingers hovering above the controls as though unsure whether to move them. His mind replayed the recent near-miss, the pings of the enemy sonar echoing in his memory. He couldn't shake the nagging feeling that he had missed something—a crucial detail that might have cost them everything.

The screen in front of him displayed their plotted course, a thin, fragile line threading through uncharted dangers. To anyone else, it might have looked flawless, but to Green, every mark on the map seemed to scream its potential for disaster.

"Stop overthinking it," came a firm voice behind him.

He turned, startled, to find Emily Carter standing there, her expression a mix of understanding and determination. She folded her arms across her chest, tilting her head slightly as though she could read his thoughts.

"We made it through," she continued, her voice low but steady, like the ocean itself. "Focus on the next step. That's all that matters now."

Green exhaled sharply, the tension in his chest loosening slightly. He nodded, his lips twitching into something resembling a grateful smile. "Thanks. I'll keep that in mind."

Carter's stern expression softened into a brief but encouraging smile. "Good," she said, before turning back to her station.

Her presence was like a lighthouse in a storm, a beacon of calm amid the turmoil. For the younger officers, she was a grounding force, her unflinching composure a reminder that fear was a luxury they couldn't afford. She had learned long ago that the only way to survive was to channel fear into focus, to keep moving forward even when the shadows of doubt loomed largest.

The *Oregon* continued its silent glide through the icy depths, its engines reduced to a whisper. Every creak of the hull, every faint echo from the vastness outside was scrutinized. In the sonar room, Carter and Petty Officer Daniels remained locked on their screens, their ears attuned to the subtlest changes in the water.

"We're in the clear for now," Daniels murmured, but his tone lacked confidence.

"'For now' is all we ever get," Carter replied, her eyes narrowing as she adjusted the filters on the hydrophone. "Stay ready."

Meanwhile, in the engine room, Boatswain Joe Landry moved among his team with the quiet authority of a man who had seen it all. He checked each system meticulously, his hands running over the controls as though they were an extension of himself. The tension in the room was thick, but Landry's steady presence kept it from tipping into chaos.

"She's holding steady," one of the engineers said, their voice almost reverent.

"She'd better," Landry muttered, his grizzled face breaking into a faint grin. "I don't plan on being crushed like a tin can today."

His comment earned a few subdued chuckles from the team, a brief but welcome reprieve from the oppressive atmosphere. Landry knew the value of moments like these—they didn't break the tension, but they made it bearable.

In the control room, King's gaze flicked to the clock, marking the passing minutes with an almost obsessive precision. Time felt distorted in the depths, each second dragging on yet slipping away too quickly.

"We're not out of the woods yet," he murmured to himself, though the sentiment was shared by all.

The *Oregon* was a shadow in the depths, unseen but not unnoticed. The patrol vessel might have moved on, but the hunt wasn't over. Every decision, every adjustment felt like a gamble, a delicate balance between survival and discovery.

For now, they pressed forward, navigating the darkness with a resolve that bordered on defiance. The ocean was vast, but their path was perilously narrow.

Part 7: The Silent Routine

Time aboard the *Oregon* began to blur, hours melting into days as the submarine pressed forward in its covert journey. The crew settled into a precise, almost mechanical rhythm, each member hyper-focused on their responsibilities. Meals were brief and functional, conversations kept to a minimum. The faint hum of the submarine's systems was omnipresent, a constant reminder of the fragile equilibrium keeping them alive.

The silence was not born of complacency but necessity. Every movement, every action had to be measured, deliberate, as if the *Oregon* itself demanded absolute discipline. The crew worked with the quiet efficiency of a well-tuned machine, but beneath the surface, the strain was palpable.

In the engine room, Boatswain Joe Landry was in his element. The tight confines of the space were filled with the rhythmic clatter of machinery and the occasional hiss of steam. Landry moved with the ease of a man who had spent decades surrounded by metal and noise. His hands worked deftly, adjusting valves and checking gauges, every motion practiced and purposeful.

He found solace in action, his mind at peace when his hands were busy. For Landry, the engine room was more than a workplace; it was his sanctuary. Here, he could channel his tension into something tangible, something he could control.

Around him, the younger sailors moved with a mix of determination and nervous energy. They watched him closely, drawn to his unshakable confidence, his steady demeanor. To them, Landry was more than a superior—he was a touchstone, a reminder of what experience and resilience looked like.

One of the younger crew members, a wiry sailor named Harris, hesitated before approaching. He had been wrestling with the growing tension for days and finally mustered the courage to speak.

"Bo'sun," Harris began, his voice low, almost uncertain. "You've been on missions like this before, right?"

Landry paused in his work, straightening up as he wiped his hands on a grease-stained rag. He regarded Harris for a moment, his sharp eyes narrowing slightly.

"Plenty," he replied gruffly, his voice carrying the weight of countless missions. "But none quite like this." He gestured vaguely around the room, as if the submarine itself could explain. "You don't just wander into Soviet waters and come out unscathed. This isn't a training drill, kid. It's the real deal."

Harris swallowed hard, his expression a mix of admiration and unease.

Landry's gaze softened slightly, and he clapped Harris on the shoulder, a rare gesture of reassurance. "You do your job, keep your head down, and pray the captain knows what he's doing. And for what it's worth, Captain King does."

The younger sailor nodded, standing a little straighter. Landry turned back to the machinery, his voice rumbling over his shoulder. "Stick with me, kid. We'll get through this."

In the sonar room, the atmosphere was equally intense. Lieutenant Emily Carter worked tirelessly, her eyes fixed on the monitor as streams of data scrolled across the screen. The occasional ping of distant sonar echoed faintly, each one scrutinized with relentless precision.

Petty Officer Daniels sat beside her, adjusting filters and calibrating equipment. "It's quiet out there," he muttered, not looking up from his controls.

"Too quiet," Carter replied, her tone clipped but thoughtful. "Quiet isn't safe. It just means they're waiting."

Daniels didn't argue. He had learned to trust Carter's instincts; they had saved the crew more than once.

Meanwhile, in the navigation bay, Thomas Green poured over their route. The young officer was meticulous, recalculating every point, every angle. The maps spread before him were etched with potential hazards—underwater ridges, thermal layers, patrol patterns. Each one was a puzzle piece, and it was his job to make them fit.

Green's brow furrowed as he marked another adjustment. He had always prided himself on his precision, but the stakes here were unlike anything he had faced before.

"Don't wear yourself out," came a voice from behind. Carter stood there, her presence commanding yet calm.

"Just making sure we don't miss anything," Green replied, his voice tinged with exhaustion.

"You won't," she said firmly. "But you'll be useless if you burn out. Trust the process. You're not alone in this."

Her words, simple but sincere, gave Green the moment of clarity he needed. He nodded, a faint smile flickering across his face before returning to his work.

As the *Oregon* continued its journey, the crew's silent routine became both their strength and their burden. The submarine moved like a phantom through the icy depths, every member of the team an essential cog in the intricate machine. They knew the risks, but they also knew each other.

And in that unspoken trust, they found the resilience to keep going.

Part 8: Unexpected Discovery

As the *Oregon* crept toward the designated coordinates for their surveillance operation, the cold, dark ocean pressed heavily against its steel hull. Inside, the tension was palpable, the crew acutely aware that they were venturing deeper into hostile waters. Conversations had ceased entirely, replaced by the low hum of machinery and the occasional creak of the submarine under immense pressure.

In the sonar room, Lieutenant Emily Carter's sharp eyes scanned the incoming data streams. She leaned closer to her console, her brow furrowing as a faint, irregular signal flickered across the hydrophone's feed. At first, it seemed like oceanic noise—perhaps interference from the natural currents—but then it repeated. A rhythm, subtle but undeniable.

Her fingers flew over the controls, isolating the signal and amplifying it. The sound filled her headphones, faint but consistent, unlike anything she'd encountered before. It wasn't civilian chatter, nor did it match the known patterns of Soviet naval transmissions.

"Captain," Carter called, her voice cutting through the quiet hum of the control room. Though calm, there was an urgency in her tone that drew immediate attention. "I've picked up an unidentified signal. It's faint but consistent—and irregular. Could be encrypted communication."

Captain King strode to her station, his movements deliberate and composed despite the flicker of concern in his eyes. He stood over her shoulder, his gaze fixed on the oscillating pattern of the readout. It was faint, almost ghostly, but its consistency was undeniable.

"Encrypted," he repeated, his tone thoughtful. "Could be a Soviet relay, a hidden listening post—or something entirely different."

He turned toward Lieutenant Green, whose steady hands hovered over the navigation controls. "Plot us a course closer to the source, but keep us within the thermocline. I don't want to give them anything to detect."

Green nodded, immediately adjusting their trajectory. His calculations were precise, each movement of the controls a delicate balance between caution and curiosity. The *Oregon* shifted course, gliding silently through the cold depths, its presence masked by the natural distortion of the thermocline layer.

The control room fell into a tense silence. Every creak of the hull, every flicker on a monitor seemed louder, heavier, as if the submarine itself was holding its breath. The signal grew stronger as they approached, its rhythm steady but enigmatic.

"Signal strength increasing," Carter announced, her hands deftly manipulating the dials. Her eyes darted across the screen as she analyzed the frequencies. "Definitely encrypted—and stationary. It's coming from a fixed location, likely a Soviet installation."

Her words hung in the air like a thunderclap. The implications were clear: this wasn't just another reconnaissance mission anymore. They had stumbled upon something significant, something hidden, and possibly something critical to Soviet operations.

King's jaw tightened, his mind racing through the possibilities. A hidden relay station? An underwater listening post? Or perhaps something even more dangerous? Whatever it was, they couldn't turn away now.

"This changes the game," he muttered, more to himself than anyone else.

King straightened, addressing the crew with the authority of a man who understood the weight of every word. "Maintain observation. No sudden moves. I want as much data on this as we can gather without compromising our position."

Carter nodded, her focus unwavering as she began recording the signal. Her hands moved with practiced precision, isolating key frequencies and logging patterns.

Nearby, Green adjusted their course incrementally, keeping the *Oregon* steady and concealed within the thermocline. His breathing was measured, his concentration absolute.

In the engine room, Joe Landry kept his team on high alert, ensuring that every system ran flawlessly. "No room for errors now," he muttered to one of his engineers. "This is where it gets real."

As the *Oregon* crept closer to the source, the air inside the submarine seemed to grow heavier. The crew's collective anticipation was palpable, their focus sharp. They knew the stakes had just risen dramatically. This wasn't merely a matter of avoiding detection anymore—it was about uncovering a hidden piece of the enemy's puzzle while remaining unseen themselves.

Outside, the ocean remained a silent, indifferent void. Inside, the *Oregon* moved like a shadow, its crew united in purpose, knowing that every decision from this moment on could mean the difference between success and disaster.

Part 9: The Trap in the Depths

The mysterious signal Carter had detected grew stronger, more defined, yet no less enigmatic. It was no ordinary radio transmission; that much was certain. Each new fragment of data hinted at something far more complex—an active source that defied simple classification. Was it a submerged beacon? A hidden Soviet base? In the dim glow of the control room, the air felt electric, charged with a tension that made even the most seasoned sailors uneasy.

At the navigation station, Lieutenant Green leaned over his console, the glow of the screen reflecting off his furrowed brow. His voice was tight as he broke the silence.
"Captain, we're nearing the signal's origin. Based on our projections, it's located roughly 200 meters below and slightly to the east."

Captain King, standing at the central console, didn't look away from the screen. His expression was unreadable, but his jaw was set with determination. "Hold our current depth," he ordered curtly. "Carter, lock onto that signal and begin recording everything. If there's any data to gather, we can't afford to miss it."

Carter's fingers flew over her keyboard, isolating the frequencies and beginning the recording process. The signal filled her headphones—an intricate sequence of rhythmic codes, strange and almost musical in its cadence. It was mesmerizing, but also unsettling, like an alien song echoing from the abyss.

Her sharp intake of breath broke the quiet. "Captain," she said, her voice cutting through the tense air. "This isn't just a radio transmission. There's something else layered in the background. Faint sonar echoes—patterned. This could be a beacon... or part of an underwater network."

King's brow furrowed at her words. A network? That meant interconnected systems—and the very real possibility that their presence might already be known.

"If it's a network," he said slowly, "it could have detection capabilities. Landry, I need a status report on our noise signature."

In the engine room, Boatswain Landry's hands moved deftly over his controls, checking the systems with practiced efficiency. Without looking up, he replied, "We're clean, sir. But if we move any closer, we risk leaving a noise trail they could pick up. These waters amplify everything."

King's mind raced. The decision before him was fraught with peril. To retreat now would mean abandoning the mission—an unacceptable outcome, given the potential significance of the signal. But pressing forward meant walking a razor's edge, risking not only their discovery but also the lives of everyone on board.

He turned back to the crew, his voice firm and steady. "Advance slowly. No more than one knot. Minimize all non-essential noise."

The order was met with swift compliance. The engines hummed at an almost imperceptible level as the *Oregon* inched forward, each movement deliberate and controlled.

In the control room, the atmosphere grew heavier with every passing second. The soft whir of instruments and the occasional creak of the hull under pressure seemed deafening in the silence. Every member of the crew was hyper-focused, their eyes darting between monitors and readouts.

Green adjusted their trajectory with painstaking care, his fingers steady despite the sweat forming on his brow. Carter remained locked on her station, fine-tuning the recording equipment to capture every nuance of the signal.

The *Oregon* moved like a shadow through the icy depths, its stealth unmatched but its vulnerability undeniable. Outside, the ocean was an endless, oppressive black, its cold embrace offering no solace. Inside, the crew clung to their discipline, knowing that one misstep could turn their covert mission into a death sentence.

"Signal strength increasing," Carter announced quietly, her voice cutting through the tension like a knife. "We're almost on top of it."

King nodded, his gaze fixed on the sonar display. The faint echoes Carter had mentioned were now more pronounced, their patterns forming a rhythm that hinted at something engineered, something deliberate.

"Eyes on everything," he said, his voice low but commanding. "We're not taking any chances."

The *Oregon* pressed onward, creeping ever closer to the source of the signal. Every creak, every breath, every flicker of light felt magnified in the stillness, a reminder that the abyss around them held dangers they could not yet see.

And though they didn't know it yet, they were approaching the heart of a trap far more intricate and deadly than they could have imagined.

Part 10: Unexpected Contact

As the *Oregon* closed in on the signal's coordinates, tension gripped the control room. Carter's sharp eyes flicked across the monitors, deciphering the shifting data. Suddenly, the faint sonar echoes she had been tracking morphed into something far more substantial. The rhythmic blips became clearer, sharper, until the outline of a long, massive object materialized on the sonar screen.

Her breath hitched. "Captain," she called, her voice steady but filled with urgency. "We have a contact. It's not just a beacon—it's a submarine. Judging by the size and signature... it's the *Sokol*. A Soviet hunter."

The words hung in the air like a thunderclap. The control room froze. The *Sokol* was infamous—a predator designed specifically to seek and destroy vessels like theirs. It wasn't just a submarine; it was a threat of the highest order.

Captain King moved quickly to Carter's station, his eyes narrowing as he examined the sonar feed. The silhouette of the *Sokol* was unmistakable, its form lying in wait like a dormant beast in the depths.

"Have they detected us?" he asked, his voice calm but carrying the weight of command.

"Not yet," Carter replied, her hands deftly adjusting the hydrophone's sensitivity. "But if we move closer or if they initiate an active search, they'll find us."

King straightened, his mind working through the options. There was no margin for error. This wasn't a moment for bold action; it was one for absolute precision. He turned to Landry, whose experienced hands hovered over the engine controls.

"Engines to stop. Full silence. We'll observe," King ordered.

"Aye, sir," Landry replied crisply, immediately cutting the engines.

The *Oregon* eased to a halt, suspended in the icy depths like a phantom. The hum of its systems fell to a whisper, leaving the submarine eerily quiet. On the sonar screen, the *Sokol* remained motionless, its presence a looming specter in the black void.

Inside the control room, every creak of the hull, every flicker of a monitor felt amplified. The crew barely dared to breathe, each moment stretching into eternity.

"Carter, record everything," King commanded. "I want a full log of their movements. Green," he turned to the young navigator, "be ready for an emergency maneuver. If we're detected, I need you sharp."

"Yes, sir," the two officers replied in unison, their voices steady despite the growing tension.

Minutes dragged on, the silence broken only by the faint hum of the hydrophone and the soft clatter of Carter's hands on her controls. She worked tirelessly, isolating frequencies and logging data.

"The *Sokol* remains stationary," she finally reported, her voice soft but sure. "They're not aware of us."

King allowed himself a brief exhale, his shoulders relaxing ever so slightly. "Good. We'll collect the data and withdraw. Let's not push our luck."

Green began plotting a cautious retreat, his hands moving deftly over the controls. But just as the *Oregon* began to inch backward, a new signal blipped onto the sonar. Carter's head snapped up, her heart pounding as she processed the data.

"Captain," she said, her voice tight with urgency. "New contact—Soviet patrol boat, closing fast. They're conducting a sweep."

The room went still again, the weight of the situation bearing down on every soul aboard. The *Sokol* might not have detected them, but the patrol boat was another matter entirely.

"Distance?" King demanded.

"Two kilometers and closing," Carter replied, her fingers flying across the console.

King's jaw tightened. The time for silence and subtlety had passed. Their position was about to be compromised.

"Green, prepare for evasive maneuvers," King ordered, his voice cutting through the tension. "Landry, bring engines to one-quarter. Carter, keep tracking the *Sokol* and that patrol boat. If we're engaged, I need every advantage."

The *Oregon* began to move, its engines humming softly as it navigated the black waters. The chess match had become a race for survival.

As the patrol boat closed in, the crew worked with a precision born of necessity. Every command, every action was executed flawlessly, the *Oregon* slipping through the depths like a shadow. Yet the weight of the moment pressed down on them all. They were no longer just gathering intelligence—they were fighting to stay alive.

And somewhere out there, the *Sokol* waited, its silence as menacing as the dark ocean that surrounded them.

Part 11: The Escape

Captain King's mind raced, calculating their options in a heartbeat. The control room was tense, the weight of the situation pressing down on every member of the crew. Outside, the ocean seemed darker, heavier, as the patrol boat's sonar swept methodically through the water.

"Green," King commanded, his voice cutting through the silence like a blade. "Immediate turn, starboard 30 degrees. Landry, engines at one-third power. Begin a dive to maximum depth. We're leaving."

Green's hands flew to the controls, the young navigator moving with precision despite the adrenaline coursing through his veins. "Aye, Captain," he replied, adjusting their trajectory.

The *Oregon* shifted its course, descending into the abyss with deliberate care. Landry monitored the engines closely, his eyes darting between the gauges. The faint hum of the machinery was the only sound, a quiet rhythm against the oppressive silence of the deep.

In the sonar bay, Carter's fingers gripped the edges of her console, her knuckles white. The patrol boat's sonar pings grew louder, more invasive. She adjusted the hydrophone, isolating the signals.

"They've begun active searching," she reported, her voice low but steady. "We're directly in their path."

King's jaw tightened, his gaze locked on the sonar display. The patrol boat was too close, its presence a tangible threat. He knew there was no room for error.

"All systems to silent mode," he ordered. "Kill engine noise. Move by inertia only. We need to slip past their scanning range."

The control room fell into an eerie stillness. The hum of the engines faded into silence, leaving only the creak of the hull as the *Oregon* coasted forward on momentum alone. The crew held their breath, their movements slow and deliberate. Even the simplest action felt dangerous.

Carter's headphones were filled with the piercing blare of the patrol boat's sonar. The signals were relentless, searching for any sign of life in the depths. She adjusted the sensitivity, tracking the boat's movements.

"They're closing in," she whispered. The tension in her voice was mirrored in every face around her.

Seconds dragged into eternity as the *Oregon* drifted, a shadow in the vast expanse. The patrol boat's sonar pings passed dangerously close, their echoes reverberating through the submarine's systems. Every creak of the hull felt like a shout in the silence.

Landry's hands hovered over the controls, ready to respond at a moment's notice. His team exchanged nervous glances, their training battling against the primal fear of detection.

King stood motionless, his presence a steadying force. His eyes never left the monitors, his mind calculating their every move. He knew that even the smallest misstep could lead to disaster.

Then, slowly, the sonar signals began to fade. The patrol boat's sweep moved further away, its focus shifting elsewhere. Carter exhaled a breath she hadn't realized she was holding.

"Signals decreasing," she said, her voice carrying the faintest hint of relief. "We're out of their scanning range."

A collective sigh of relief rippled through the control room, but it was short-lived. King's expression remained stern, his voice cutting through the momentary reprieve.

"Don't relax yet," he warned. "We're not out of danger. Maintain silent running. Green, hold course and prepare for the next phase."

The crew snapped back to focus, their brief relief replaced by the grim determination to see the mission through. The *Oregon* continued its retreat, slipping further into the safety of the depths.

But everyone aboard knew the truth: this was only the beginning. The enemy wasn't finished hunting, and their escape was far from guaranteed.

Part 12: The Captain's Decision

The *Oregon* settled at a safer depth, its hull creaking softly under the weight of the ocean. The faint hum of the submarine's systems was the only sound, punctuating the heavy silence in the control room. Captain King stood at the central console, his gaze distant but sharp, as though peering into the challenges that lay ahead.

One by one, the key officers assembled around him. Carter, Green, and Landry exchanged brief glances, each of them acutely aware that the captain's next decision could define the outcome of their mission—and their survival.

King broke the silence, his voice low but resolute. "That was too close," he began, his eyes scanning the faces before him. "We've gathered substantial data for analysis, but I have a feeling we haven't seen everything this place has to offer. If we leave now, we complete our mission safely. But if we stay... what's the risk?"

Carter was the first to speak, her tone measured but firm. "The risk is significant. We're deep in Soviet-controlled waters, and the longer we linger, the higher the chance of encountering additional patrols. They've already come close once. If they sweep back, they'll be more thorough."

Green shifted, his brow furrowed as he considered her words. "I agree, but Captain, if we leave now, we might miss something vital. That signal we detected—it's not random. It could be linked to a hidden base, maybe even a critical relay station. It's worth investigating further, especially since we're already here."

Carter cast a sharp look at Green, but she didn't argue. Both points had merit, and the tension between caution and curiosity hung heavy in the air.

King listened in silence, his expression unreadable. His mind worked through the variables: the value of the intelligence they'd gathered so far, the potential for further discovery, and the ever-present threat of detection. Every decision carried weight; every choice had consequences. Finally, he straightened, his voice cutting through the tension.

"We'll stay," he said, his tone firm but calm. "Two more hours. No longer. Carter, I want every scrap of data you can collect—frequencies, patterns, anything. Green, keep us in a holding position, but be ready to move at a moment's notice. Landry, ensure all systems are primed for an emergency evacuation."

The officers nodded, their respect for King's measured decision evident in their swift compliance. No one voiced disagreement, though the gravity of the choice was clear in their faces.

As the crew returned to their stations, the atmosphere aboard the *Oregon* grew heavier. The submarine remained a shadow in the depths, its presence masked by the thermocline. Every member of the crew worked with quiet precision, aware that these two hours might tip the scales between success and catastrophe.

In the sonar bay, Carter adjusted her controls with meticulous care, isolating faint signals and logging every detail. Her focus was unshakable, her sharp mind analyzing patterns in the static.

At the helm, Green kept his hands steady on the controls, his attention split between the navigation console and the sonar readout. His earlier confidence had been tempered by the close encounter, but his resolve was stronger than ever.

In the engine room, Landry moved among his team like a commander on a battlefield, his gravelly voice issuing clear, concise instructions. The systems were running smoothly, but Landry knew better than to trust the calm before the storm.

King remained in the control room, his eyes flicking between the monitors and the officers under his command. He could feel the weight of their trust, their faith in his decisions. It wasn't a burden he took lightly.

Time seemed to crawl as the *Oregon* hovered in its concealed position. The faint blips of distant sonar signals echoed through the hydrophone feed, each one a reminder of the enemy's proximity. Every second stretched taut with tension, a balancing act on the razor's edge of discovery.

Finally, Carter broke the silence. "Captain, we're picking up new patterns in the signal. This... this could be significant."

King leaned closer, his jaw tightening. "Log everything. We'll evaluate later. For now, stay sharp."

The *Oregon* held its position, its crew united in quiet determination. The line between risk and reward was razor-thin, but under King's steady leadership, they pressed forward, knowing that their mission demanded nothing less.

Part 13: The Signal's Warning

The faint, rhythmic pulse Carter had been recording suddenly began to shift, its tempo and tone evolving into something more deliberate, more purposeful. It was subtle at first—a minor fluctuation in frequency—but it was enough to catch her sharp, trained ear. Leaning closer to her console, Carter adjusted the filters, isolating the emerging pattern.

Her fingers flew over the keyboard, her focus narrowing as the signal transformed. Then it struck her—a realization that sent a chill racing down her spine.

"Captain," she called, her voice tight, "the signal is changing. This isn't random anymore. It's coordinated—deliberate. I think we're intercepting an encoded directive. It could be relayed to nearby vessels."

King turned sharply, his eyes locking on her as his mind processed the implications. "Is it targeted at us?" he asked, his voice steady but weighted with urgency.

Carter hesitated, her brow furrowed as she rechecked the data. "Not directly, but if they're aware of an intruder in the area, this could initiate a patrol sweep."

Green swiveled in his chair, his expression a mix of concern and urgency. "Captain," he said, "if that's a directive for the *Sokol* or another unit, we might be running out of time. They could mobilize within minutes."

King's jaw tightened, his eyes narrowing as he quickly weighed their options. Every decision was a gamble now, a balance between gathering critical intel and ensuring the safety of his crew.

"Maintain full silence," King ordered, his voice cutting through the tension in the control room. "Carter, keep monitoring the signal and log every detail. If this is a communication relay, we need to know its purpose."

He turned to Green. "Plot an alternate course out of the area. I want an escape route ready if we need it, but do it quietly. No sudden movements."

"Aye, Captain," Green replied, his hands already moving over the navigation controls, plotting a cautious yet efficient exit.

"Landry," King continued, his gaze shifting to the bo'sun, "prep the engines for immediate maneuvering. We might need to move fast."

Landry nodded, his expression grim but focused. "Understood, sir. I'll keep the engines at minimal output until you give the word."

The control room descended into a tense, methodical silence. Every crew member worked with the precision of a well-oiled machine, each movement deliberate and controlled. The faint hum of the submarine's systems seemed almost deafening against the quiet, a reminder of the delicate balance they maintained.

Carter's hands didn't stop, her attention locked on the evolving signal. She could see it now—a structured pattern buried within the noise, its purpose clear to her trained eyes. The message wasn't random; it was tactical, and its implications were chilling.

"It's spreading," she said quietly, her voice steady despite the unease gnawing at her. "The signal's range is increasing. It's pinging across multiple frequencies, likely relaying between vessels."

King's face darkened. "They're coordinating," he muttered, more to himself than to the crew. "This isn't just a sweep—they're preparing for something bigger."

The submarine's instruments showed no immediate threats, no sudden changes in the patterns of nearby vessels, but the air inside the *Oregon* felt heavier with each passing second. Every creak of the hull, every flicker of the monitors seemed magnified in the oppressive stillness.

King stood at the center of it all, his presence a steadying force amid the mounting tension. He knew the risks they faced, knew how close they were to the edge. But retreating too soon could mean leaving vital information behind—intel that could define the success or failure of their mission.

"Stay focused," he said, his voice firm but calm, addressing the entire control room. "Every second counts. Let's make sure this wasn't all for nothing."

The crew nodded, their resolve solidifying under his leadership. The *Oregon* remained a shadow in the depths, poised between discovery and escape, its fate hanging by a thread of precision and discipline.

Part 14: The Edge of Discovery

As the *Oregon* began its cautious retreat, a faint yet unmistakable signal flickered to life on the sonar screen. At first, it was just a whisper—an anomaly at the edge of their detection range. But it grew clearer with each passing second, resolving into the steady rhythm of an approaching vessel.

Carter's eyes narrowed as she leaned into her console, isolating the new contact from the ambient noise. Her fingers hovered over the controls, adjusting the filters with practiced precision.

"Captain," she called, her voice calm but urgent. "We've got movement. Bearing zero-nine-zero, closing at approximately five knots. It's deliberate."

The control room fell silent, every head turning toward the captain. King's expression hardened, his mind racing through the possibilities. A patrol sweep? A random search? Or something worse—an intentional pursuit?

"Landry," King said sharply, turning to his trusted bo'sun, "what's our noise profile?"

Landry didn't look up from his console as he answered, his voice steady but laced with tension. "Clean, sir. We're silent. But if they're running active sonar, it's only a matter of time before they find us."

King's jaw tightened, the faint creak of the hull under pressure mirroring the weight of the decision he had to make.

"Helmsman," he said, his tone decisive, "descend to 300 meters. We'll use the deeper thermocline as cover. Keep it slow and steady—no room for mistakes."

"Aye, Captain," the helmsman replied, his hands moving deftly over the controls.

The submarine began its descent, the engines humming softly as it slipped deeper into the ocean's embrace. The hull groaned faintly under the increasing pressure, a haunting reminder of the forces at play. The dim lighting in the control room cast long shadows across the crew's faces, their focus unbroken as they monitored every detail.

Outside, the waters darkened into an inky void, the *Oregon* becoming a shadow among shadows. The thermocline—a natural layer where water temperature and salinity shifted—offered a fragile sanctuary, distorting sonar signals and masking their presence. But it was a temporary refuge, and everyone aboard knew it.

"Carter," King said, his voice cutting through the tense silence, "keep tracking that vessel. If it's the *Sokol*, I want confirmation before they even get a hint of us."

"Yes, sir," Carter replied, her hands moving with steady precision. She adjusted the sensitivity of the hydrophone, isolating the approaching signal. Her focus was razor-sharp, her breathing controlled despite the growing tension.

The faint blip on the sonar screen became more defined—a moving shadow that seemed to glide through the depths with deliberate intent.

"It's maintaining course," Carter reported, her voice low but clear. "No active pings yet. They're either scanning passively or already know exactly where to look."

Green, stationed at the navigation console, glanced at the screen and frowned. "If they're closing in, Captain, they've either got a lead or they're sweeping blind. Either way, we're running out of room to maneuver."

King's gaze didn't waver as he responded. "We'll give them no reason to suspect. Maintain silence. Landry, be ready to cut all systems if necessary. Carter, keep feeding me updates."

Landry nodded, his fingers poised over the controls. "Understood, sir. We're ready to go dark on your command."

The submarine continued its descent, the ambient noise of the deep ocean pressing in around them. Every sound, every flicker on the monitors was magnified by the crew's heightened awareness. The shadow on the sonar grew closer, its presence a silent specter in the depths.

The *Oregon* moved with the precision of a predator, its crew attuned to the delicate dance between stealth and survival. Every action was deliberate, every decision calculated.

"Captain," Carter said, breaking the tense silence, "they've altered course slightly. It's subtle, but they're closing the gap."

King's jaw set. The hunt was far from over, and the stakes had never been higher.

Part 15: Unseen Threats

The *Oregon* settled at 300 meters, its hull groaning faintly under the relentless weight of the sea. The thermocline's interference wrapped around the submarine like a fragile shield, distorting the hostile sonar signals. For a fleeting moment, the crew dared to believe they had evaded pursuit. The tension in the control room eased slightly, breaths coming a little easier.

But the reprieve was short-lived.

Carter's sharp intake of breath cut through the silence like a knife. Her eyes darted across the sonar readout, and her hands tightened on the console.

"Captain," she said, her voice barely above a whisper. "We've got a secondary contact. Stationary. Bearing one-eight-zero." She hesitated before adding, "It could be another Soviet asset."

King's gaze snapped to the monitor, his jaw tightening as he took in the faint but undeniable data. A second presence—silent and unmoving—hovered at the edge of their detection range.

"They're boxing us in," Green muttered, his voice low, the weight of realization settling over him like a shroud.

"Not yet," King said, his tone cutting through the rising anxiety like steel. He turned to Carter. "Confirm if the second contact is active."

Carter's fingers flew across the controls, isolating the faint signal. The hydrophone feed crackled softly as she refined the parameters. "No movement detected, sir," she said after a moment. "It's either a submerged beacon or a docked vessel. No active sonar, no propulsion signatures."

King's expression remained grim. "Let's hope it stays that way," he replied, his voice calm but edged with resolve.

"Helmsman," King ordered, his eyes fixed on the display, "adjust course to zero-seven-zero. I want distance between us and both contacts. Make it slow and quiet—no sudden moves."

"Aye, Captain," the helmsman replied, his hands moving steadily over the controls.

The *Oregon* began its deliberate maneuver, the engines humming softly as the submarine glided deeper into the void. Every movement was calculated, each adjustment precise. The margin for error was nonexistent.

The control room was heavy with silence, save for the faint whir of machinery and the rhythmic blips of sonar. The crew moved with the practiced efficiency of seasoned operators, but the tension was palpable. Each of them felt the immense pressure—not just of the ocean surrounding them, but of the unseen enemies lurking in the darkness.

Landry monitored the engines with an eagle eye, his fingers hovering over the controls like a pianist poised to strike the keys. The stress etched lines into his weathered face, but his hands never wavered.

In the sonar bay, Carter continued her analysis, her mind racing as she considered the implications of the second contact. A submerged beacon? A docked submarine? Each possibility carried its own set of dangers.

Green spoke quietly, his voice breaking the stillness. "If it's docked, what are the odds it has active surveillance equipment?"

Carter glanced at him, her expression unreadable. "High," she admitted. "But without movement or active sonar, we can't confirm. For now, it's just a threat in waiting."

"Every shadow in these waters feels like a threat," Landry muttered under his breath, his eyes never leaving his station.

King remained silent, his gaze fixed on the monitors. The data painted a grim picture, but his resolve was unshaken. He had navigated worse odds before—and he wasn't about to falter now.

The submarine pressed on, its crew unified by a singular focus: survival. The faint outline of the stationary contact loomed in the background, a silent reminder of the dangers that surrounded them. The *Oregon* moved like a phantom, a shadow slipping through the depths, its presence masked by the thermocline's distortions.

Each passing second felt like an eternity, the weight of the mission pressing down on every soul aboard. Yet under King's command, the *Oregon* advanced—carefully, deliberately—toward whatever awaited them in the dark.

Part 16: A Captain's Resolve

Time in the depths felt elastic, stretching unbearably thin as the *Oregon* crept through the labyrinth of perilous waters. Hours bled into what felt like days, each second marked by the faint, ghostly pings of the *Sokol* and the ominous, stationary presence of the secondary contact. The tension in the control room was suffocating, like the very ocean pressing in against the hull.

Captain King stood at the helm, a steadfast figure amidst the quiet turmoil. His eyes moved across the instruments with relentless focus, each flicker of data etched into his mind. He was the fulcrum on which the crew's confidence balanced—a quiet strength in the face of the unknown.

Behind him, Lieutenant Green hesitated, then finally spoke, his tone careful but insistent. "Captain, we've been holding position for hours. If they know we're here, this could turn into a trap. Should we consider aborting the mission?"

King didn't respond immediately. His gaze shifted to the map spread across the console, his fingers tracing the precise route they'd navigated. The plotted course shimmered faintly under the dim lights, a reminder of the intricate dance they'd undertaken.

"We stay," he said finally, his voice steady and unyielding. He looked up, meeting Green's eyes with the clarity of unwavering resolve. "Until we have concrete evidence that they're aware of us, we proceed. This mission isn't over until we've done what we came here to do."

The room remained silent, the weight of his words settling over the crew like the cold of the depths. They exchanged brief glances—fear was there, yes, but so was respect. King's confidence was their anchor, and in the oppressive void of the ocean, it was a lifeline.

"Carter," King continued, turning his attention to her, "resume data collection on the first signal. I want every detail logged and cross-referenced."

"Yes, sir," she replied, her fingers already moving swiftly over her console.

"Landry," King said next, his voice firm but calm, "ensure the engines are primed for an immediate dive. If this turns into a pursuit, I want no delays."

"Aye, Captain," Landry replied, his focus as sharp as his captain's.

"Green," King finished, "keep monitoring their movements. If they so much as twitch, I want to know about it."

"Yes, sir," Green answered, his fingers steady as they hovered over the navigation controls.

The *Oregon* remained motionless, a predator biding its time in the icy depths. Its crew worked in tense, methodical silence, each task executed with the precision of a finely tuned instrument. The stakes had never been higher, and every decision carried the weight of survival.

For a moment, the only sounds were the faint hum of the submarine's systems and the rhythmic beeping of the sonar. But then, without warning, the sonar console emitted a sharp ping—a sound that sliced through the silence like a blade.

Carter's head snapped up, her eyes fixed on the monitor as new data streamed across the screen. Her breath caught as the realization struck her.

"Captain," she said, her voice tight with urgency. "We have a direct contact. It's *Sokol*. They're active—and heading straight for us."

The room seemed to contract, the air thick with adrenaline. King's face hardened, his mind calculating at a pace that outstripped the growing tension.

"Dive to 400 meters," he barked, his voice cutting through the room like a commandment. "All hands to silent running. We're about to find out if they really know we're here."

The crew sprang into action. Green adjusted their trajectory with swift precision, the submarine angling downward into the cold embrace of deeper waters. Landry issued rapid commands to his team, ensuring the engines maintained the barest whisper of output.

"Depth at 350 meters," Green reported, his voice steady despite the chaos.

"Maintain descent," King ordered.

The *Oregon* slid into the void, its movements ghostlike. The hull creaked under the mounting pressure, a sound that reverberated through the submarine like a whispered warning. Every member of the crew held their breath, the silence broken only by the faint blips of sonar and the hum of their systems.

On the sonar screen, the *Sokol*'s signature loomed larger, its intent unmistakable. Carter's hands moved with lightning speed, tracking its movements and isolating its signals.

"They're sweeping actively now," she reported, her voice tight but composed. "If we're not careful, they'll pick us up in the next pass."

King's jaw set, his expression unreadable. He turned to his crew, his voice calm despite the storm brewing around them. "Hold your positions. Stay focused. We've been here before, and we've come out on top. We'll do it again."

The crew nodded, their resolve strengthening under his leadership. The *Oregon* continued its silent retreat, a shadow slipping through the abyss, its crew braced for the next move in a deadly game of cat and mouse.

Part 1: The Unwelcome Shadow

The control room of the USS *Oregon* was shrouded in a tense silence. The faint glow of monitors and instrument panels illuminated the focused faces of the crew. Each of them understood the gravity of their mission, but the stakes had just escalated dramatically. The Soviet submarine *Sokol*, a hunter-killer designed to track and destroy vessels like theirs, had entered the area—and it was heading straight for them.

"Captain," Lieutenant Carter's voice was steady, though a flicker of unease crept into her tone, "I'm picking up a direct contact. It's *Sokol*. Active sonar is confirmed. They're running a sweep."

"How far out?" Captain King's voice was calm but carried a commanding edge.

"Three kilometers, bearing zero-eight-five," Carter reported, her eyes glued to the sonar display. "Speed: five knots. They're descending."

The room felt colder, the weight of her words sinking in. King straightened, his eyes narrowing as he considered their options.

"Helmsman, take us down to 400 meters," he ordered. "Landry, cut all non-essential systems. Full silent running."

"Aye, sir," the helmsman responded, his hands moving swiftly over the controls. The *Oregon* began its descent, its hull groaning under the increasing pressure of the depths. The lights in the control room dimmed further as non-critical power systems were shut down, leaving the space bathed in an eerie, muted glow.

"Silent running initiated," Landry confirmed, his gruff voice breaking the silence. "Engines at minimum output. Noise profile is clean."

King nodded, his mind already racing through possible scenarios. "Good. Hold this course and speed. Let them come to us—we'll use the thermocline as cover."

The thermocline, a natural boundary layer in the ocean where temperature and salinity changed, distorted sonar waves and created a blind spot. It wasn't foolproof, but it was their best chance to avoid detection.

The crew moved with precision, every action deliberate and soundless. The faint hum of the sonar filled the control room as the *Sokol*'s pings grew louder. Each pulse reverberated through the hydrophones, a relentless reminder of the predator closing in.

Petty Officer Daniels sat at the sonar station, his headphones clamped tightly to his ears. His fingers hovered over the controls, ready to adjust for any changes in the signal.

"They're scanning aggressively," he murmured, his voice low. "Wide beam, high intensity. They're looking for something."

Carter glanced at her monitor, her sharp eyes analyzing the data. "Captain, their depth is now 350 meters. They're closing in on the thermocline."

King's expression remained unreadable, but the tightening of his jaw betrayed his concern. The Soviets weren't just patrolling; they were hunting. He turned to Green.

"Mr. Green, plot an emergency course to 450 meters if needed, but hold steady for now," King said. "Let them come closer—we stay quiet."

"Yes, sir," Green replied, his voice steady as he adjusted the navigation system.

The *Oregon* hung in the depths like a ghost, invisible in the dark ocean. The creaks and groans of the hull under pressure were the only sounds, a stark reminder of the hostile environment surrounding them. Every crew member was acutely aware that one mistake—a single noise or miscalculation—could reveal their position and spell their end.

Carter's voice cut through the tense silence. "Captain, *Sokol* has slowed to three knots. They're holding position just outside the thermocline."

King frowned, his brow furrowing in thought. "They're testing us. Waiting for a reaction."

Green shifted uneasily in his seat. "If they hold that position, they could force us deeper. We can't stay down here indefinitely."

King's gaze remained fixed on the sonar display. He knew Green was right. The longer they stayed in the *Sokol*'s vicinity, the greater the risk of detection—or worse, entrapment. But moving now would be just as dangerous, if not more.

"We wait," King said firmly. "They haven't found us yet. If we stay quiet, they might assume the area is clear."

The crew exchanged glances, their faith in their captain unwavering despite the mounting tension. The *Oregon*'s fate rested on his decisions, and they trusted him to guide them through the perilous situation.

As the minutes dragged on, the oppressive silence pressed down on everyone. The pings from the *Sokol* continued, steady and unrelenting. Carter monitored the signals with laser focus, her fingers poised over the controls.

"They're not moving, sir," she reported. "But they're maintaining an active sweep."

"Good," King said, his voice calm. "Let them waste their energy. We'll outlast them."

But as he stared at the dimly lit sonar screen, a part of him knew this encounter was far from over. The Soviets were too skilled, too determined. This was only the beginning of the deadly game that was unfolding beneath the icy waters of the Barents Sea.

Part 2: The Predator Approaches

The pings from *Sokol's* sonar grew louder, each one reverberating through the hydrophones like the steady beat of a heart. In the sonar room, the atmosphere was stifling with tension. Petty Officer Daniels sat rigid at his station, his headphones firmly in place as he adjusted the dials with precise movements. His brow furrowed in concentration as he worked to track the Soviet submarine's every move.

"They're scanning aggressively," Daniels murmured, his voice barely above a whisper, as though speaking louder might give away their position. "Wide beam, high intensity. They're serious about finding something."

The steady rhythm of *Sokol's* sonar pulses echoed ominously through the hydrophone, growing sharper with each passing moment. Daniels tilted his head slightly, listening intently before continuing, "If they sweep just a little lower, they might catch our shadow."

Across the room, Lieutenant Carter's sharp eyes darted between her displays. Her fingers hovered over her console, ready to act. She spoke with practiced calm, though her tone betrayed the weight of the situation. "Captain, their course is shifting. They're descending. Depth: 350 meters."

King stood tall at the center of the control room, his expression unreadable, but his mind raced with calculations. The Soviets were closing in, and their descent toward *Oregon's* depth was no coincidence. It was a deliberate maneuver, the kind of probing behavior that suggested they suspected an intruder. His options were narrowing with each passing second.

"Helmsman, hold at 400 meters," King said, his voice calm but firm. "We stay hidden in the thermocline."

The thermocline was their lifeline—a natural barrier created by differing layers of temperature and salinity. It distorted sonar signals, making it difficult for enemy vessels to detect anything beyond its boundary. It wasn't a perfect shield, but it was their best chance to remain invisible.

"Aye, sir," the helmsman responded, his hands moving swiftly over the controls. The *Oregon* stabilized at 400 meters, the hull groaning softly under the pressure of the deep.

The control room fell into an uneasy silence, broken only by the faint hum of *Sokol's* sonar and the occasional creak of the submarine's hull. Each sound seemed amplified in the confined space, magnified by the crew's heightened senses.

Petty Officer Daniels adjusted his headphones again, trying to discern more details about the approaching threat. The steady pinging of the *Sokol* filled his ears, relentless and unforgiving.

"They're getting closer," he reported in a hushed tone. "Range: 2.5 kilometers."

Carter kept her focus on the data scrolling across her screens. She noted the gradual adjustments in *Sokol's* speed and heading, confirming their methodical search pattern. "They're thorough," she said quietly, almost to herself. "They're not leaving anything to chance."

King's gaze shifted to Carter. "Any indication they've locked onto us?"

"Not yet, sir," Carter replied. "Their signals are wide, and they're running patterns. No direct ping on our position so far."

King nodded, though his mind was already running through potential contingencies. The Soviets were clearly skilled and cautious, the hallmarks of a crew trained to anticipate and neutralize threats. He couldn't afford to underestimate them.

As the minutes dragged on, the tension in the control room grew palpable. Every creak of the submarine's hull under the crushing weight of the ocean felt like a betrayal, threatening to give away their presence. The crew remained silent, each member acutely aware of the stakes.

Daniels broke the silence with another update. "Depth holding at 350 meters. They're maintaining a steady descent."

King turned to Green, his navigator. "Maintain current course and depth. We don't move unless we have no choice."

Green nodded, his hands steady on the navigation console. "Understood, sir."

The faint glow of the control room's instruments cast an eerie light over the faces of the crew. Each of them knew the gravity of their situation. They were being hunted, and the hunter was closing in.

"Captain," Carter said suddenly, her voice cutting through the quiet. "*Sokol* is adjusting their sweep angle. They're focusing downward."

King's expression hardened. The Soviets were narrowing their search, moving closer to *Oregon's* position within the thermocline.

"Hold steady," he ordered, his voice steady despite the growing tension. "Let them make the first move."

The *Oregon* remained motionless in the dark, a silent shadow hidden within the ocean's depths. The stakes were clear: survival depended on their ability to remain unseen. Every decision, every sound, and every second mattered.

Part 3: The Unseen Danger

The minutes crept by with agonizing slowness. Each second felt stretched, drawn taut by the tension that gripped the crew. The relentless pings of *Sokol's* sonar echoed through the hull of the *Oregon*, a rhythmic drumbeat that seemed to vibrate in their bones. In the oppressive silence of the control room, every creak of the submarine and every faint beep of the instruments felt magnified, each sound a potential betrayal.

Carter broke the silence, her voice sharp but measured. "Captain, *Sokol* has stopped its descent. Depth: 370 meters. They're holding position."

Captain King stood near the sonar console, his hands clasped behind his back, his expression impassive. He didn't respond immediately, his gaze fixed on the sonar screen where the faint blip of *Sokol* lingered like a predator circling unseen prey. Finally, he spoke, his tone even but laced with calculation.

"They're waiting. Fishing for us to make a mistake."

The room felt as though it held its breath, the crew listening intently to their captain. Lieutenant Green, seated at the navigation console, looked up, concern etched across his face.

"If they hold there, sir, they could pin us down," Green said, his voice low. "Force us deeper. We can't outlast them forever at this depth."

King shifted his gaze to the map table, his fingers tracing the plotted course in silence. He knew Green was right. The pressure at their current depth was unrelenting, both on the vessel and the crew. Yet any sudden movement could betray their presence. They were cornered, and the Soviets knew it.

"We don't move unless we have no choice," King finally said, his voice resolute. "They think there's something here, but they don't know for sure. Let them waste their time. They'll tire eventually."

The faint hum of the *Oregon's* systems filled the void, a fragile soundscape in the oppressive stillness. Every member of the crew remained laser-focused on their stations, their nerves wound tightly. They had trained for moments like this, but training couldn't prepare them for the raw tension of being hunted by one of the Soviet Navy's deadliest submarines.

Carter kept her eyes locked on her screen, scanning for even the faintest changes in *Sokol's* position or behavior. She spoke without looking up. "Their sonar sweep has slowed, Captain. They're narrowing their beam."

King's jaw tightened imperceptibly. He understood the tactic—*Sokol's* crew was attempting to refine their search, focusing their instruments to locate the *Oregon* with greater precision. The Soviets were meticulous, patient. This wasn't a random sweep; it was a calculated hunt.

Time dragged on, the weight of it pressing heavily on the crew. They all knew that the longer they remained in *Sokol's* vicinity, the greater the risk. The Barents Sea was vast, but not infinite. The Soviets would likely have backup assets in the area—patrol boats, aircraft, or even another submarine. Each passing minute brought the possibility of reinforcements closer.

King turned to Landry, who stood by the engineering console, his expression as stoic as ever.
"Status report," King said.

"Engines holding steady, sir. Noise profile remains clean. But we're pushing the limits of silence." Landry hesitated, then added, "If they close the gap, it'll be harder to stay hidden."

King nodded. He appreciated Landry's blunt honesty. There was no room for false optimism here. He returned his gaze to the sonar screen, watching the faint blip of *Sokol* as it hovered, waiting.

The silence was broken again by Daniels, his voice tense but controlled. "They're holding their depth, but their speed has increased slightly. Could be repositioning."

"Or baiting us," Carter muttered under her breath, her hands never leaving the controls.

King weighed his options carefully. Every instinct told him to stay put, to let the Soviets make the first move. But he also knew the dangers of prolonged inactivity. The ocean was not a forgiving place, and the *Oregon* was as much at risk from its own circumstances as it was from the enemy.

He made his decision.
"Hold position," he said firmly. "They're testing the waters, but they're still uncertain. We don't give them a reason to confirm their suspicions."

For now, the *Oregon* remained a silent shadow in the depths, hidden within the cold, concealing layers of the thermocline. The crew held their positions, their breaths shallow and movements deliberate. But they all knew this fragile balance couldn't last forever. Time was not on their side, and *Sokol* was a predator that wouldn't leave without a kill—or a conclusion.

Part 4: A Silent Duel

The *Oregon* sat in absolute stillness, a phantom suspended in the vast darkness of the ocean depths. Its engines were silent, its crew unmoving. Every man and woman aboard held their breath as the pings of *Sokol's* sonar began to diminish, their sharp echoes growing fainter. The oppressive tension in the control room lightened ever so slightly, though no one dared to fully believe it was over.

"Distance: increasing," Carter reported, her voice steady but carrying a faint note of relief. Her eyes remained locked on the screen, where the blip representing *Sokol* was gradually drifting further away. "They're moving north, Captain."

A rare moment of calm flickered across Captain King's face. He exhaled softly, the sound barely audible in the silence of the room. "Good," he said, though his voice was firm with caution. "But stay on alert. This could be a feint."

The words hung in the air like a warning bell. The crew knew the *Sokol*'s reputation; it was not a submarine that gave up easily. A feigned retreat could be a tactic to bait them into movement, revealing their position.

The control room remained bathed in dim light, the crew's focus unwavering. Each officer kept their eyes fixed on their instruments, monitoring the slightest changes. The tension was palpable, the silence between the fading pings almost louder than the sounds themselves.

Carter adjusted her console, her fingers quick and precise. "Pings are fading into background noise," she said. "But I'm maintaining tracking. If they reverse course, I'll pick it up immediately."

King nodded, his gaze never leaving the tactical display. "Helmsman, hold position. I don't want us moving an inch unless it's necessary."

"Yes, sir," the helmsman replied, his voice low and controlled as he kept the *Oregon* perfectly steady.

Time stretched on, the faint hum of the submarine's systems the only sound in the room. The *Sokol's* blips grew more distant, merging with the ambient noise of the ocean. For the crew of the *Oregon*, the relief was fleeting. They had seen moments like this before—a predator disappearing into the shadows, only to strike when least expected.

King's instincts screamed that the danger wasn't over. His gut told him the *Sokol* wasn't abandoning its hunt; it was merely changing its strategy. He turned to Carter.
"Keep them in your sights. If there's any deviation in their course or speed, I need to know immediately."

"Yes, Captain," Carter replied, her voice calm but focused. Her eyes remained glued to her screen, her fingers poised to react.

Minutes passed in tense silence. The control room felt like a coiled spring, the crew ready to act at the slightest sign of danger. The faint pings of the *Sokol* had nearly disappeared now, leaving an eerie quiet in their wake. Yet no one dared to relax, least of all King.

"Mark their last known position," King ordered. "If they're doubling back, we'll be ready."

The *Oregon* remained motionless, a hunter itself, lying in wait in the cold, dark ocean. The duel wasn't over; it had only paused, each side waiting for the other to make the next move.

Part 5: The Feint Revealed

The tension in the control room was finally beginning to lift. The fading pings of *Sokol's* sonar had almost disappeared, and the crew allowed themselves the smallest reprieve. Breaths were steadier, and even the oppressive silence seemed to loosen its grip. But just as a fragile calm settled, Carter's console lit up, the sharp beeping of a new signal cutting through the stillness like a blade.

Her eyes widened as she scanned the incoming data, her fingers darting over the controls to verify the readings. The moment she spoke, the faint hope in the room vanished.

"Captain," she said urgently, her voice slicing through the air. "*Sokol* has turned back. They're accelerating—directly toward us. Distance: two kilometers and closing fast."

All heads turned to the captain. King's expression hardened, his features carved from stone. He moved closer to the tactical display, his sharp gaze assessing the situation.
"They're probing for us," he said grimly. "Testing the waters. Helm, prepare for a silent dive."

The helmsman's hands moved swiftly, readying the submarine for a deeper descent. King turned to Carter, his tone clipped but calm. "Confirm their speed."

"Seven knots and rising," she replied without hesitation, her voice steady despite the tension that electrified the air. "They're running active sonar again."

The control room erupted into focused urgency. Officers relayed orders in hushed voices, their movements quick but deliberate. The dull hum of the submarine's systems was punctuated by the sharp, rhythmic pings of *Sokol's* sonar, now growing louder with each passing second. This was no longer a game of cat and mouse—it was an outright hunt.

"Take us to 450 meters," King ordered firmly, his voice cutting through the controlled chaos. "Maintain silent running. We won't outrun them, but we can outmaneuver them."

The helmsman acknowledged the order, his hands deftly adjusting the controls. The *Oregon* began its descent, the angle slight but deliberate. The groaning of the hull under the increasing pressure reverberated through the submarine, a constant reminder of the hostile environment surrounding them.

As the submarine descended, the control room was bathed in the dim glow of its instruments, each screen displaying critical information. The crew worked with mechanical precision, their training and discipline carrying them through the palpable tension.

Carter's voice broke the quiet.
"*Sokol* is holding at 370 meters but closing fast. They're sweeping aggressively. If they adjust their depth, they'll intersect our position."

King nodded, his mind racing. Every decision now was a gamble, every action a potential revelation of their location. He leaned over the sonar display, watching the *Sokol's* relentless approach.
"They're trying to force us to reveal ourselves," he muttered. "But we're not giving them anything."

The submarine crept deeper into the abyss, the faint creaks of the hull almost drowned out by the rising pings of the Soviet sonar. The thermocline had concealed them thus far, but King knew it wasn't an impenetrable shield. The *Sokol* was skilled, its crew methodical. Any mistake now could spell disaster.

"Status on noise profile," King asked, his tone calm but commanding.

"Minimal, sir," Landry replied from the engineering station. "Engines are running clean. No anomalies."

"Good," King said. "Maintain current protocols. Carter, any changes in their behavior?"

"They've adjusted their heading slightly, Captain," Carter responded, her eyes locked on her console. "It's subtle, but they're aligning with our last known position."

The captain's jaw tightened. *Sokol* wasn't just searching—it was stalking.

The seconds felt like hours as the *Oregon* continued its descent. The crew remained locked in their stations, their focus unbroken. Every sound, every flicker of an instrument carried weight. The oppressive darkness of the depths pressed in from all sides, but the submarine pressed on, a shadow among shadows.

Carter's voice broke the silence again.
"They're now within 1.5 kilometers, Captain. Their active sonar is targeting our depth."

King's mind worked like clockwork, analyzing every possibility. "Helm," he ordered, his voice steady as ever, "adjust heading ten degrees to port. Keep it gradual. Carter, monitor their response."

The *Oregon* shifted its course ever so slightly, the movement so smooth it was almost imperceptible. The captain's gamble was simple: avoid a direct encounter by maneuvering quietly and using the natural distortions of the ocean to their advantage.

The room remained tense, the faint hum of the submarine's systems a backdrop to the relentless pings of *Sokol's* sonar. The crew understood the stakes; their lives depended on their ability to remain unseen and unheard.

Carter's voice came again, this time with a note of urgency. "Captain, *Sokol* is accelerating again. Distance: one kilometer."

King's gaze remained fixed on the tactical display.
"Hold steady," he ordered. "We let them make the first move. They don't know we're here—not yet."

The *Oregon* hung in the depths, silent and unseen, but the duel was far from over. Each passing moment brought them closer to the edge, the outcome balanced precariously on a knife's edge.

Part 6: A Narrow Escape

The *Sokol* bore down on them, its sonar pings echoing through the hydrophones with relentless intensity. Each burst of sound seemed to reverberate through the *Oregon's* hull, growing louder with every passing moment. The atmosphere in the control room was suffocating, tension so thick it felt like a physical presence. Every crew member sat rigid, their eyes darting between monitors and instruments, searching for signs of imminent danger.

Captain King stood rooted in place, his posture calm but his focus razor-sharp. His mind worked methodically, processing the escalating threat with the precision of a seasoned tactician. He understood that every second mattered now.

"They're almost on top of us," Carter said, her voice barely above a whisper. Her hands hovered over her controls, steady but poised to react. "Distance: 500 meters and closing."

The room seemed to hold its breath. The sonar pings were now deafening, each one a stark reminder of how perilously close the *Sokol* had come to finding them. The *Oregon* was trapped in the hunter's net, and the crew knew it.

King's voice broke the silence, calm yet commanding. "Green, adjust course ten degrees starboard. Landry, engines at one-sixth power. Let's slip past them—slow and quiet."

"Yes, sir," Green replied immediately, his hands moving over the navigation controls. Landry acknowledged the order with a curt nod, his experienced hands making precise adjustments to the engines. The *Oregon* began a subtle shift in course, its movements almost imperceptible.

The submarine crept through the dark ocean like a shadow, its engines so quiet they were nearly silent. Every vibration, every creak of the hull felt amplified in the oppressive stillness. The crew's movements were deliberate, their breaths shallow. No one spoke; no one dared to break the fragile silence.

Carter's eyes remained locked on her console, monitoring the *Sokol's* position with unwavering focus. The Soviet submarine continued its search, its sonar pings sweeping across the water with relentless precision. On the screens, the two vessels appeared perilously close, their paths almost overlapping.

King's eyes flicked between the sonar display and his crew. He could see the strain etched into their faces, but he also saw their discipline. They trusted him, and he would not let them down.

Minutes dragged on like hours as the *Oregon* inched away, its course just wide enough to avoid direct detection. The sonar pings of the *Sokol* were deafening in the hydrophones, each one a hammer blow against the crew's nerves. The tension was almost unbearable, the crew acutely aware that the smallest mistake—a sudden noise, an incorrect maneuver—could betray them.

Finally, Carter's voice broke the silence, still quiet but tinged with relief. "They've missed us," she reported. "The *Sokol* is continuing north. Distance: increasing."

The room collectively exhaled, the sound of dozens of held breaths released at once. The oppressive weight of the moment began to lift, though the tension lingered like a shadow.

King allowed himself a brief nod of satisfaction, though his expression remained serious. "Good work, everyone," he said. His voice carried a quiet pride, a steady reassurance. "Maintain course and stay silent until they're well out of range."

The *Oregon* glided further into the depths, its movements slow and deliberate. The crew began to settle back into their stations, though the edge of vigilance remained sharp. They had survived, but the danger was far from over.

In the control room, King's gaze lingered on the tactical display, watching as the *Sokol*'s signal grew fainter. His instincts told him this was only the beginning of their trials. For now, though, they had evaded the predator, slipping through the jaws of danger by the narrowest of margins.

"Carter," King said, his tone calm but firm, "keep tracking them until they're completely out of range. Green, plot a course to deeper waters. We're not taking any chances."

"Yes, sir," came the unified responses. The crew's discipline was unshaken, their focus absolute.

The *Oregon* remained a silent shadow in the deep, its crew prepared for whatever lay ahead.

Part 1: Troubling Detection

The low hum of the *Oregon's* systems filled the submarine's engineering section, a rhythmic background sound that normally faded into the subconscious of its crew. But in the control room of the reactor, the hum was disrupted by the sharp chirp of an alarm. Red warning lights began to blink on the panels, casting an ominous glow over the tense faces of the engineers.

Chief Engineer Landry leaned over the console, his experienced hands moving quickly to assess the situation. His eyes narrowed as he examined the readouts—fluctuations in coolant pressure, erratic at first but growing increasingly unstable. The implications hit him immediately, his stomach tightening as he turned to the intercom.

"Bridge, this is Engineering," Landry said, his voice calm but urgent. "We're registering coolant pressure irregularities in the reactor system. Potential overheating is imminent if we don't act now."

In the control room, Captain King's brow furrowed as he processed Landry's report. The tension that had just begun to ease after their narrow escape from the *Sokol* returned in full force. A malfunction in the cooling system was a nightmare scenario, particularly at their current depth. The risks of exposure or even a catastrophic failure were unthinkable.

"Landry, what's the severity?" King asked, his tone sharp but steady.

"We're not at critical levels yet," Landry replied over the intercom, his voice carrying a hint of strain. "But the pressure's dropping fast. If it continues, we could be looking at a reactor overheat within the hour."

King nodded, already issuing orders. "Carter, update me on sonar activity. Any signs of enemy movement?"

Carter's fingers flew over her console as she scanned the latest data. "I'm picking up faint sonar echoes, Captain," she reported. "Could be distant patrols. Nothing close enough to pinpoint us yet, but we can't rule out the possibility."

King's jaw tightened. The *Oregon* was caught between two equally deadly threats: the danger of discovery by nearby Soviet patrols and the internal hazard of a failing cooling system.

"Green, take us down an additional 20 meters," King ordered. "Landry, initiate manual control of the coolant system. Keep all operations silent. I don't want a single decibel out of place."

"Yes, sir," came Landry's clipped reply.

The submarine descended slightly, its hull groaning softly under the increasing pressure. In the engineering section, Landry directed his team with precision, their movements practiced and efficient despite the high stakes. The room was hot, the hum of machinery punctuated by the occasional hiss of steam as they worked to stabilize the system. Landry's hands flew over the manual controls, adjusting valves and pressure levels in a delicate balancing act to keep the reactor in check.

Back in the control room, Carter continued monitoring sonar activity. The faint echoes persisted, their intermittent rhythm suggesting the presence of Soviet vessels, though still distant. Each blip was a reminder of the ever-present threat above.

"Sonar signals remain faint, Captain," Carter said. "But they're consistent. If they're running a grid search, we could be in their path."

King's face remained unreadable, but the weight of the situation was clear. "Understood," he said. "Maintain silent running. All non-essential systems remain offline. We'll handle this one step at a time."

The room was silent but for the soft hum of the instruments. The crew worked with quiet urgency, their movements deliberate and their focus unwavering. They understood the stakes: a single error could mean the end for them all.

As the engineers in the reactor room continued their efforts, Landry's voice came over the intercom again. "Captain, we've managed to stabilize pressure temporarily, but it's a patch, not a solution. The system will hold for now, but we need to implement a full repair as soon as it's safe."

King nodded, his mind racing. "Good work, Landry. Stand by for further instructions."

Turning back to his crew, King's voice carried authority and determination. "We're not out of this yet. Stay sharp, stay quiet, and let's keep this under control. We'll see it through."

The *Oregon* continued its slow, silent glide through the depths, its crew locked in a battle against both the ocean and the clock. The stakes were higher than ever, and every decision would determine whether they lived to fight another day.

Part 2: Pinpointing the Problem

The engineering bay hummed with urgency, every sound amplified by the stakes hanging over the *Oregon*. Red indicator lights cast shifting shadows on the walls, mirroring the intensity of the crew's movements. The low, rhythmic hiss of the systems intermingled with the occasional metallic clang as tools were hurriedly grabbed and used.

Chief Engineer Landry was at the center of the storm, his commanding voice cutting through the tense atmosphere.
"Focus, people," he barked, his eyes scanning the control panel like a battlefield general surveying the terrain. "We're looking for a block in the coolant system. Narrow it down—now."

The team moved with practiced efficiency, but the tension in the air was palpable. Ensign Walker was crouched near a valve cluster, his face slick with sweat as he worked a manual override. Sparks flew as he pried open a stubborn housing, revealing the inner workings of the critical system.

"Pressure's still erratic," Walker called out, his voice tight. "Looks like something's constricting flow between pump two and exchanger four."

"That's our choke point," Landry replied immediately, his tone sharp and decisive. "Confirm the readings on exchanger four. If it's blocked, we need to isolate it."

Petty Officer Allen, stationed at the adjacent control terminal, tapped furiously on her console. "Flow rates confirm it, Chief. There's a significant drop in coolant output. Something's lodged in the exchanger."

Landry didn't hesitate. "Alright, here's the plan," he said, his voice steady but urgent. He pointed to Walker. "You're on pump diagnostics. Check the intake side for debris or buildup. Allen, focus on the exchanger itself—run a bypass simulation to see if we can route around the block without a full shutdown. This needs to be precise, or we risk overloading the system."

The engineers exchanged quick nods, their determination cutting through the suffocating heat of the room. Landry turned back to his station, his hands moving with practiced precision as he monitored the coolant pressure levels. Each adjustment was like walking a tightrope—too much force, and the entire system could spiral out of control.

"Let's move, people," he urged. "This isn't just about fixing the system—it's about keeping us alive."

Meanwhile, in the control room, Carter sat at her station, her fingers dancing over the sonar console. The faint blips of potential enemy vessels still lingered in the background, their rhythm steady but unnervingly persistent.

"Captain," she said, breaking the silence, "the sonar echoes are holding steady, but there's a subtle shift in their pattern. It's like they're repositioning."

King's gaze sharpened. "Define 'repositioning.'"

"They're not moving toward us directly," Carter explained, her voice clipped but calm. "But it's as if they're aligning for a broader sweep. If we create any significant noise, they'll pick it up instantly."

King's jaw tightened. "Understood. Keep tracking them and let me know if their behavior changes. Landry's team is under enough pressure without an external complication."

Back in the engineering bay, the air felt heavier, the combination of heat and stress pressing down on the team. Walker wiped his forehead with the back of his glove as he peered into the pump assembly.

"Chief, I've got partial debris buildup in the intake line," he reported. "Looks like it's clogging the primary flow path."

Landry nodded, his mind already formulating the next steps. "Clear it out manually," he ordered. "And be careful. Any sudden pressure shift could spike reactor temps."

"On it," Walker replied, reaching for his tools.

Allen's voice cut through the noise. "Bypass simulation complete, Chief. We can reroute coolant flow temporarily, but it's going to strain the auxiliary pumps. If those fail…"

"They won't," Landry interrupted, his voice firm. "Not on my watch. Implement the bypass, but monitor the output every five seconds. If there's even a hint of instability, we shut it down and reassess."

Minutes stretched into what felt like hours as the team worked, the temperature in the bay rising alongside the stakes. Every sound—the hiss of steam, the clang of a wrench, the faint hum of the reactor—felt like a ticking clock counting down to disaster.

In the control room, Carter's voice cut through the tension once more. "Captain, sonar echoes are holding steady. No direct movement, but they're not retreating either."

King nodded, his expression unreadable. "Good. Keep monitoring. We can't afford any surprises."

Landry's voice came through the intercom next, calm but carrying the weight of urgency.
"Captain, we've identified the block and initiated a bypass. The system's stabilizing, but this is temporary. We've bought ourselves some time, but not much."

King's response was immediate. "Understood, Landry. Good work so far. Keep me updated on any changes. And keep it quiet—we're not out of this yet."

The *Oregon* remained a silent predator in the depths, its crew working tirelessly against the clock. Above them, the ocean waited, indifferent to their struggle.

Part 3: Racing the Clock

The control room was tense, the dim lighting reflecting the mood of the crew. Even the hum of the *Oregon's* systems felt heavier, more oppressive, as though the submarine itself knew what was at stake. On one of the screens, a gauge began to climb, its needle inching toward the red zone with an almost deliberate slowness.

"Captain," Carter reported, her voice carefully neutral. "Reactor temperature is rising. Not critical yet, but... we're headed there."

King didn't flinch, though the news landed like a punch. He straightened, his gaze sweeping over the room. "All right, everyone," he said, his voice calm but carrying the weight of command. "This isn't the time to panic. It's the time to focus. And above all, it's the time to be quiet. We're trying to avoid both a meltdown and a Soviet welcoming committee, so let's keep the decibels lower than Landry's usual complaining."

A faint ripple of chuckles broke the tension, just enough to let the crew breathe. Landry's voice came through the intercom almost immediately. "For the record, Captain, my complaints are entirely justified. Unlike this coolant system, I work under constant pressure."

Down in the engineering bay, Landry's team was moving with the urgency of a pit crew at a high-stakes race. The air was thick with heat, stress, and the faint metallic tang of coolant vapor. Landry himself stood at the center, his sleeves rolled up and his voice cutting through the din like a drill sergeant.

"Walker, how's that intake looking?" he barked, wiping sweat from his forehead with a grease-streaked hand.

Walker, crouched by the pump assembly, muttered something unintelligible before raising his voice.
"Almost there, Chief. This thing's tighter than a jar of pickles on a bad day."

"Less commentary, more fixing," Landry shot back, though there was a flicker of amusement in his tone.

Meanwhile, Allen was hunched over her terminal, her fingers flying across the keys. "Bypass pathway is ready for manual rerouting, Chief. But I'll need someone to keep an eye on the auxiliary pumps—those things are finicky."

"Finicky? Allen, those pumps are held together with duct tape and sheer willpower. Of course they're finicky." Landry pointed to Walker. "You're on pump babysitting duty after you clear that intake."

In the control room, Carter's sonar console lit up with a soft ping. She leaned forward, her brow furrowing as she analyzed the data. "Captain, faint echoes at three kilometers. It's consistent with their previous pattern, but it's closer than before."

King's jaw tightened. "Not what I wanted to hear, Carter. Keep tracking them. Let me know the second they change speed or heading."

Turning to Green, King issued his next order.
"Green, adjust our position. I want us tucked as deep into the thermocline as possible without moving more than we need to."

Green nodded, his hands already working the controls. "On it, sir. Just enough to keep us out of sight and out of mind."

"Good," King replied, his voice steady. "Let's make this submarine as invisible as Landry is at morning briefings."

Back in engineering, the team was fully in motion. Walker finally pulled a twisted piece of metal out of the intake valve, holding it up triumphantly like a fisherman showing off his catch.
"Here's your culprit, Chief. A rogue gasket piece clogging the line."

Landry didn't even look up. "Great. Frame it later. For now, put the valve back together and move. We're rerouting coolant manually."

The team sprang into action, their movements synchronized like a well-rehearsed dance. Allen monitored the auxiliary systems, calling out adjustments as Landry and Walker worked to reassemble the intake and reroute the flow. The heat in the bay was stifling, sweat dripping from their faces as they worked against the clock.

"Pressure's stabilizing, but it's touchy," Allen warned. "If the aux pumps hiccup—"

"They won't," Landry interrupted, his tone leaving no room for doubt. "Not if we do our jobs."

In the control room, the tension was palpable. Carter's sonar pings continued their steady rhythm, a haunting reminder of the Soviet vessels hovering nearby. The reactor temperature gauge was no longer climbing, but it hovered dangerously close to the red zone.

"Landry," King called through the intercom. "What's your status?"

"We've got the coolant rerouted," Landry replied, his voice strained but determined. "System's stabilizing, but it's a bandaid on a bullet wound, Captain. It'll hold for now, but we're still in trouble if those Soviets get any closer."

King allowed himself a small exhale. "Good work, Landry. Keep it quiet and keep it stable. We'll deal with the rest when we're out of the frying pan."

Turning back to his crew, King spoke with calm authority. "We've bought ourselves time. Let's make the most of it. Stay sharp, stay quiet, and remember—we're not out of this yet."

The *Oregon* continued its slow glide through the depths. Inside, its crew fought to maintain control, their determination unyielding. Outside, the ocean and the unseen enemy waited, patient and indifferent.

Part 4: Coordinated Actions

The engineering bay buzzed with focused activity, though any unnecessary noise was replaced by gestures and whispered exchanges. The air was thick—not just with heat, but with the weight of what was at stake. Every movement seemed to carry extra gravity, every breath carefully measured. Landry stood at the center of it all, a maestro conducting an orchestra of sweat-soaked engineers.

"All right, people," Landry whispered, keeping his voice low but firm. "We're not just fixing a coolant system—we're dancing around a hornet's nest. One wrong move, and we're the ones getting stung."

Walker crouched near a tangle of valves, his tools clinking softly as he worked. He gestured toward a line of piping with one hand while making a slicing motion across his neck with the other—a clear "shut it off" signal. Allen nodded from across the room, her fingers flying across her console as she rerouted flow paths.

"Pressure's holding steady," Allen murmured, her voice barely audible. "But we're at the limit, Chief. Auxiliary pumps are carrying the load, but if they so much as hiccup..." She didn't finish the sentence. She didn't need to.

"They won't hiccup," Landry whispered back. His voice, though quiet, carried unshakable conviction. "Not if we give them a smooth ride. Walker, how's that valve looking?"

Walker gave a thumbs-up, his face streaked with grime and sweat. He mouthed the word "clear" before moving to the next section.

Above them, in the control room, the atmosphere was equally tense. Carter's console glowed faintly as she monitored the sonar. The faint pings of an unknown vessel echoed in the background, their presence like a persistent mosquito hovering just out of reach.

"Captain," Carter whispered, leaning toward King. "I'm still picking up faint sonar echoes. No changes in speed or heading, but they're steady— closer than I'd like."

King nodded, his face unreadable but his mind racing. "How close are we talking?"

"Too close for comfort if we make any noise," she replied, her fingers never leaving the console.

King turned to the rest of the crew. "All right, team. From now on, we're communicating like spies in a library. Whisper if you have to, gesture if you can. And for the love of everything holy, no one sneezes."

That last line elicited a few muted smiles, though the gravity of the situation kept the room quiet.

Back in the engineering bay, the team worked with almost choreographed precision. Landry gestured toward Allen, mimicking a twisting motion to indicate another bypass adjustment. She nodded, her hands adjusting the controls with surgical precision. Walker moved between sections like a shadow, checking each valve and pipe with a meticulousness that would have made his drill instructor proud.

"Chief," Allen whispered, glancing at her monitor. "Flow's stabilizing, but we've got some minor fluctuations near exchanger two."

"Of course we do," Landry muttered under his breath before motioning toward Walker. "Check it out. And quietly. If you drop a wrench, you're swimming back to base."

Walker stifled a laugh and gave a mock salute before disappearing into the maze of pipes.

In the control room, Carter's eyes widened slightly as her screen flickered. She motioned toward King, pointing at a series of sonar blips.

"They're holding position," she whispered. "But they've adjusted their sweep angle. They're narrowing their search."

King's expression didn't change, but the tension in his posture was palpable. "Hold steady," he whispered back. "If we stay quiet, we stay invisible."

Behind him, Green mimicked a slow, steady breathing motion with his hands, silently urging everyone to remain calm. The unspoken message was clear: panic had no place here.

Landry's voice crackled softly through the intercom. "Captain, flow's fully rerouted. Coolant levels are stabilizing, but we're running this system on hope and duct tape. I'd give it a 70/30 chance of holding."

King's lips twitched in what might have been a smile. "That's better odds than I was expecting. Good work, Landry. Keep it stable and keep it silent."

Back in the engineering bay, Landry turned to his team. "You heard the captain. Silent heroes, people. Let's make this look easy."

Walker grinned, his teeth flashing briefly in the dim light. "If this is easy, I'd hate to see difficult."

"Don't tempt fate," Allen shot back, her voice a bare whisper. "Fate's got a twisted sense of humor."

Even as they exchanged quiet quips, the team's hands never stopped moving, their focus unbroken. The coolant system hissed softly as the rerouted flow settled into place, and for the first time in hours, the gauges on the engineering console began to normalize.

In the control room, King straightened slightly, his sharp gaze fixed on the sonar display. The faint blips of the *Sokol*'s sonar still lingered, but they hadn't grown louder. For now, they were safe—barely.

"Maintain positions," King said softly. "We've done the hard part. Let's not blow it now."

The tension remained, but there was a faint, shared sense of relief among the crew. For the moment, they had bought themselves a fragile reprieve.

Part 5: Setbacks and Tension

The air in the engineering bay felt like it had gained weight, pressing down on the team as they worked. Sweat trickled down faces, mixing with streaks of grease and grime. The hiss of redirected coolant and the faint hum of the reactor provided a constant backdrop, punctuated only by the occasional whispered instruction.

Walker crouched near a stubborn valve, his face twisted in frustration. He gritted his teeth, twisting the handle with all his strength, but it wouldn't budge. Finally, he let out a harsh whisper, the closest thing to shouting anyone dared.

"Chief, this valve is stuck tighter than a politician's promise," Walker muttered, wiping his brow with the back of his hand.

Landry shot him a look that could have cut through steel. "Then get it unstuck. We're not exactly swimming in spare time here."

"I've tried," Walker replied, gesturing emphatically at the valve. "It's not moving. We need to force it, or this whole fix is dead in the water."

Allen glanced up from her terminal, her brow furrowed. "Forcing it could spike noise levels, Chief. If that *Sokol* out there is as close as Carter says, we might as well send them a handwritten invitation."

Landry ran a hand through his damp hair, weighing the options. His instincts screamed against creating even the smallest sound, but the clock was ticking, and the rising pressure in the coolant lines wasn't going to wait for perfect conditions.

Walker held up a crowbar-like tool he had improvised from spare parts, raising his eyebrows as if to say, *Why not?*

Landry grimaced. "Captain's call," he said finally, reaching for the intercom.

In the control room, King's voice came through clear but soft. "Status, Landry?"

"We've hit a snag, Captain," Landry replied, his voice tight with frustration. "One of the valves won't open. We're considering... unconventional methods, but there's a risk of noise."

There was a brief pause, the kind that stretched longer than it should. Finally, King responded. His voice was calm but carried the weight of the decision. "What's the likelihood of success?"

"Eighty percent it works. Twenty percent it makes a racket loud enough to wake the dead," Landry said, his tone laced with dry humor.

King exhaled quietly, his eyes meeting Carter's for a moment as she monitored the faint sonar pings. "Do it," he said firmly. "Quietly as you can, but get it done. We don't have time for perfection."

Back in the engineering bay, Landry turned to Walker with a nod. "You heard him. Make it happen, but don't break anything you can't fix."

Walker grinned, though his nerves showed in the tightness of his expression. "Don't worry, Chief. I'll finesse it."

"Finesse it with a crowbar," Allen muttered under her breath, earning a smirk from Walker as he positioned the tool.

The entire team froze as Walker began to apply pressure. The creak of metal straining against metal sounded far too loud in the confined space. Every eye was on the valve, every breath held. Finally, with a muted *pop*, the valve gave way, releasing a small hiss of coolant.

Walker looked up, his face split in a triumphant grin. "And that, folks, is why they keep me around."

Landry didn't waste a second. "Good. Allen, stabilize flow. Walker, check the next section for pressure spikes. Let's finish this before something else decides to break."

The team moved with renewed urgency, their motions efficient but precise. The heat in the bay was stifling, the constant groaning of the hull under immense pressure serving as a grim reminder of their precarious position.

In the control room, Carter glanced up from her console, her expression tense. "Captain, sonar echoes are steady, but if we make any more noise down there—"

"They're almost done," King interrupted, his voice steady. "Focus on the search pattern. If they adjust heading, I want to know the second it happens."

Carter nodded, her fingers flying across the console.

Back in engineering, Landry's voice cut through the low hum of the systems. "Final readings, Allen?"

"Flow's steady, Chief," she replied, her voice a mix of relief and exhaustion. "Auxiliary pumps are holding. We're back in business—for now."

Landry tapped the intercom. "Captain, valve's open, flow is stable. Coolant levels are back where they should be. We're in the green."

In the control room, King allowed himself a small nod. "Good work, Landry. Keep monitoring for any anomalies. And give Walker a pat on the back for me—quietly."

Walker, overhearing the comment, gave a mock bow in the engineering bay. "You hear that, Chief? I'm getting pats on the back now. Guess I'll be writing my memoirs next."

"Just fix the next valve, Walker," Landry snapped, though the corners of his mouth twitched upward.

The team got back to work, the sense of relief tempered by the knowledge that their job was far from over. For now, the coolant system was holding—but in the depths of the ocean, the line between stability and disaster was razor-thin.

Part 6: The Critical Moment

The engineering bay felt like it was holding its breath, even though the gauges finally began to show signs of stabilizing. The coolant system, though still fragile, was functioning—its soft hissing sound a tentative reassurance. Landry and his team moved quietly but efficiently, their faces set in grim determination. The tension in the air was so thick, it seemed to seep into the walls.

And then it happened.

A sudden metallic *clang* echoed through the bay, loud enough to make every head snap around. Walker froze mid-step, his face a mask of panic as he stared at the wrench he'd accidentally knocked off a console. The tool spun on the floor before settling with a final, damning clatter.

In the control room, Carter stiffened, her eyes widening as her sonar display flared to life. A new set of pings rippled across the screen—stronger, closer, and moving toward their position. Her voice was a strained whisper, but it cut through the tense silence like a blade.

"Captain, sonar activity just spiked. They're moving. Pattern suggests they're zeroing in on our location."

King's mind raced. The noise was minor, but down here, even the smallest sound carried far. His eyes locked on Carter's screen, where the faint blips of the *Sokol* had grown sharper, more deliberate. "How close?" he asked, his voice calm despite the storm brewing beneath the surface.

"Two kilometers," Carter replied, her tone clipped. "Closing slowly, but definitely closing."

The room tensed further as King considered their options. Staying still risked detection if the Soviets swept directly over them. Moving risked making more noise, potentially sealing their fate. It was a gamble either way.

"Green," King said, turning to the helmsman. "Plot a slow evasive course. Minimal engine power—just enough to drift out of their predicted sweep."

Green hesitated for only a second before nodding. "Aye, Captain. Adjusting course by five degrees, bearing south-southeast."

Down in engineering, Landry caught wind of the commotion through the intercom. He cursed under his breath, his hands gripping the edge of the console as he spoke.
"Captain, coolant flow is stable, but this system's still delicate. I'm monitoring it like a hawk, but if we push too hard—"

"We're not pushing, Landry," King interrupted. "We're gliding. Keep your team on standby in case we need another miracle."

Landry smirked grimly. "Standing by for miracles is our specialty, Captain."

Walker, still looking guilty, muttered, "Guess I'm in charge of the next one." Allen shot him a glare but said nothing, her focus back on the auxiliary systems.

The *Oregon* began its slow, deliberate shift, the engines humming at a whisper-soft level. Every creak of the hull under pressure felt deafening in the silence. Carter's eyes stayed glued to her console, tracking the Soviets' approach with an intensity that bordered on obsession.

"They're adjusting course again," she reported. "It's subtle, but they're angling toward our last known position."

"Maintain speed," King ordered, his voice steady. He could feel the weight of every decision bearing down on him. "If they're following the sound, they'll miss us if we keep moving at this rate."

The crew moved in a synchronized, almost choreographed manner, communicating through whispers and hand signals. Green's hands were steady on the controls, adjusting the submarine's pitch with painstaking care. In engineering, Landry and his team monitored the coolant system, ready to intervene at the first sign of instability.

Then Carter's voice broke through the tense quiet again. "Captain, sonar activity is increasing. I'm picking up faint secondary signals—possibly additional vessels."

King's expression hardened. One enemy submarine was bad enough. Two or more would turn their escape into an impossible maze.

"What's the distance on the second signal?"

"Four kilometers and holding," Carter said. "They're not moving toward us yet, but if they start coordinating—"

"They won't get the chance," King cut her off. "Focus on the *Sokol*. If we evade them, the others won't matter."

Time seemed to stretch endlessly as the *Oregon* drifted through the depths, the faint pings of the *Sokol's* sonar growing louder and then softer in a maddening rhythm. Every moment felt like a razor's edge, every sound a potential betrayal.

"Status, Landry?" King asked through the intercom.

Landry's voice came back, calm but resolute. "Coolant system's holding steady, Captain. But I'm not taking my eyes off it. This thing's stable, but it's like balancing on a knife—one wrong move, and it's all over."

King nodded to himself, though Landry couldn't see it. "Understood. Keep monitoring. We'll need that system to be flawless if we have to make a break for it."

The *Oregon* continued its silent glide, its crew locked in a battle of nerves against an invisible enemy. In the control room, Carter's eyes never left her screen, tracking the *Sokol's* every move. Beside her, King stood like a statue, his mind weighing every variable, every risk.

Finally, Carter exhaled softly. "They're shifting north. Sonar activity is decreasing. I think they're moving off."

A wave of relief swept through the control room, though no one dared to fully relax. King allowed himself a brief nod before turning to Green. "Maintain our course and speed. No sudden movements until they're out of range."

In engineering, Landry leaned back slightly, wiping sweat from his brow. "Walker," he said with a faint smile, "next time, try not to drop anything, huh?"

Walker chuckled nervously. "No promises, Chief."

For now, the *Oregon* had avoided disaster—but in the cold, unforgiving depths of the ocean, the line between survival and catastrophe remained perilously thin.

Part 7: Returning to Stability

The first sign of relief came not in words but in a subtle shift on the gauges. The reactor temperature, which had lingered dangerously close to critical, began its slow descent back to safer levels. The needle inched downward, almost hesitantly, as though testing the waters before fully committing. In the control room, the atmosphere was still thick with tension, but the slight reprieve was palpable.

"Temperature dropping," Carter reported, her voice softer, less strained. "Reactor stabilizing. Coolant flow is holding steady."

King, who had been standing as still as a statue, finally allowed himself to relax his shoulders. He turned toward Carter, his expression calm but with a flicker of gratitude in his eyes. "Good work, Carter. Keep monitoring. Let me know if anything changes."

Then he shifted his focus to Green. "Take us down another 15 meters. Slow and silent. If they decide to come back, I want us buried so deep they'll think twice about diving after us."

The *Oregon* began its descent, the groaning of the hull under pressure a reminder of the immense forces at play. Every adjustment, no matter how slight, felt monumental. Green's hands moved deftly over the controls, his movements deliberate, almost reverent. The submarine responded like a well-trained animal, obeying each command with precision.

In the engineering bay, Landry and his team gathered around the main console, their faces a mixture of exhaustion and satisfaction. The coolant system, which had been on the verge of collapse, now hummed with a steady rhythm. It wasn't perfect, but it was enough.

"All right, people," Landry said, his voice low but carrying authority. "We've done the hard part, but this is no time for complacency. Keep monitoring those auxiliary pumps. If one of them so much as hiccups, I want to know about it before it even thinks about failing."

Walker, still looking sheepish from earlier, gave a mock salute. "Aye, Chief. No more hiccups. And no more dropped wrenches, I swear."

Landry rolled his eyes but didn't respond. His focus was already back on the data streaming across the screens.

In the control room, Carter's attention remained fixed on her console. The faint sonar pings from the *Sokol* had diminished, fading into the ambient noise of the ocean. But she wasn't ready to declare them clear just yet.

"Sonar echoes are growing weaker," she reported. "They're moving farther north. No sign of additional vessels."

King nodded but didn't let his guard down. "Good. Let's keep it that way. Maintain silent running and hold this depth. We're not taking any chances."

The crew began to settle back into their stations, though the tension in the air hadn't entirely dissipated. Conversations were minimal, movements precise, as though any misstep might undo the fragile stability they'd worked so hard to achieve.

Landry's voice came through the intercom, breaking the silence. "Captain, coolant system is holding. Reactor temp's back in the green, but I'd recommend keeping an eye on it for the next few hours. This fix is solid, but it's not exactly factory-standard."

King allowed himself a faint smile at the dry humor. "Understood, Landry. Good work down there. Make sure your team gets some rest— you've earned it."

"Rest?" Landry replied, the sarcasm in his voice unmistakable. "Captain, I don't even remember what that is. But I'll make sure the team gets some downtime. Walker might need a nap after all the heavy lifting he's been doing."

A quiet chuckle rippled through the engineering bay, the first genuine release of tension since the crisis began. Even Walker grinned, raising his hands in mock surrender. "Hey, I got that valve open, didn't I?"

The *Oregon* continued its descent into the dark, cold depths of the ocean, its movements slow and deliberate. In the control room, King surveyed his crew, noting the exhaustion etched into their faces. These were his people—brave, skilled, and unyielding in the face of danger. He felt a swell of pride, though he kept it to himself.

"We've made it through the worst of it," King said, his voice steady but carrying a quiet intensity. "But we're not out of the woods yet. Stay sharp. Stay focused. We're not surfacing until I'm sure the only thing above us is clear skies."

The crew acknowledged the order with quiet nods, their determination unshaken. For now, the *Oregon* was safe, its systems stable, and its crew united. But the ocean held its secrets close, and the next challenge was never far away.

Part 1: The Hunter in the Shadows

The *Sokol* glided silently through the cold, black waters, its hull a dark silhouette against the faint glow of bioluminescent plankton. Inside, the tension was palpable, a simmering mix of frustration and determination that coursed through the narrow corridors of the submarine.

In the command center, Captain Vasily Kovalensko stood with his arms crossed, his piercing gaze fixed on a map of the seafloor displayed on the wall-mounted screen. His broad shoulders seemed to bear the weight of the ocean itself, yet his posture radiated unshakable confidence. A faint glimmer of steel reflected in his eyes—the look of a man who had hunted before and had no intention of letting his prey escape.

"The Americans are here," Kovalensko declared, his deep voice cutting through the murmurs of his officers like a knife. "They think they can hide from us, but the sea reveals everything. If we have not found them yet, it is only because we have not looked deeply enough."

Around him, the command staff listened intently. Lieutenant Mikhail Orlov, the sonar operator, leaned forward over his console, his fingers tapping methodically as he adjusted the sensitivity of the equipment. Beside him, Senior Engineer Tatiana Zhuravleva made rapid calculations on a notepad, her expression sharp and focused. The crew of the *Sokol* was seasoned, disciplined, and entirely loyal to their captain's vision.

"They've used the thermocline to their advantage," Orlov said, not looking up. "Their hull is built to scatter sound. If they're careful, they could pass right beneath us without a trace."

"And yet," Zhuravleva added, "sound will always betray them eventually. A propeller's resonance, a pressure fluctuation—it's only a matter of time."

Kovalensko gave a small, approving nod. "Exactly. Time is on our side. But I have no intention of waiting for it to favor us. We will force their hand."

He turned to Orlov. "Expand the sensor grid. Deploy the passive hydroacoustic net. I want every sound within twenty kilometers mapped to the nearest decibel."

Orlov hesitated. "Captain, the net is—"

"Expensive? Complex?" Kovalensko interrupted, his tone sharp but not unkind. "Both are true. But it is also effective. Do it."

"Yes, Captain." Orlov bent back to his work, already adjusting the controls to release the sensors.

The *Sokol* began its silent dance of preparation. In the belly of the submarine, engineers moved swiftly, checking the integrity of the hydroacoustic sensors as they prepared to deploy the network. The devices, sleek and lethal in their design, were capable of picking up the faintest vibrations in the water—an errant engine hum, the clink of metal on metal, even the subtle shifts of water displaced by a submarine's movement.

Above, Kovalensko paced the command center like a predator stalking its territory. The map updated in real-time, showing the expanding reach of the sensor net as the *Sokol* methodically closed off potential escape routes.

"This operation will succeed because we understand the terrain better than they ever could," Kovalensko said, more to himself than to his officers. "The ocean is our ally, our weapon. It hides us as much as it reveals them."

The final sensor was deployed with a faint *click* that resonated through the ship's systems. Orlov straightened, his voice measured but with a hint of anticipation.
"The grid is live, Captain. We'll begin receiving data in thirty seconds."

Kovalensko stopped pacing, his sharp eyes fixed on the screen as the first wave of acoustic data appeared—a series of faint ripples, like whispers in the dark. Most were natural sounds: the movement of currents, the call of distant marine life. But one anomaly caught his attention, a faint blip on the edge of the grid.

"Analyze that," he ordered.

Orlov worked quickly, filtering out the background noise. "Preliminary analysis: consistent with a man-made object. Small signature, but it's there."

"Good." Kovalensko's voice softened, a wolfish grin tugging at the corner of his mouth. "The Americans may think they are clever, but they cannot hide forever. Adjust course to intercept. The hunt begins."

The *Sokol* moved with deadly precision, its sleek form cutting through the depths like a knife. Above and around it, the hydroacoustic sensors worked tirelessly, feeding data back to the command center. Each new blip, each faint ripple in the ocean's fabric, was analyzed, cataloged, and cross-referenced.

Kovalensko remained a steady presence in the center of it all, his confidence infectious. His crew worked as an extension of his will, their movements efficient and unerring. The *Sokol* was no longer just a submarine—it was a hunter, its captain the apex predator.

As the map filled with data, the crew of the *Sokol* knew one thing for certain: the Americans were here, hiding somewhere in the shadows. And Captain Kovalensko had no intention of letting them stay hidden.

Part 2: Into the Labyrinth

The faint hum of the *Oregon*'s systems was the only sound in the tense silence of the control room. The crew moved with quiet precision, their focus sharpened by the constant threat looming just beyond the steel hull. Carter's eyes were glued to her sonar console, the soft green glow illuminating her tense features.

A sudden ping, sharper and closer than before, broke through the ambient hum. Carter's breath hitched, and her fingers danced across the controls, filtering the incoming data. Her voice, steady but tight, broke the silence. "Captain, new contacts detected. It's *Sokol*. They're deploying sensors—multiple points. They're building a grid."

King, standing at the center of the room, turned his sharp gaze toward the sonar display. The arcs of data lit up, forming a web that seemed to tighten with every second. His jaw tightened, the weight of the situation bearing down on him.
"They're trying to corner us," he muttered. "If they complete that grid, we'll be fish in a barrel."

At the navigation station, Green was already pulling up detailed maps of the seafloor. His fingers moved swiftly, highlighting topographical features—ridges, trenches, and the dense network of undersea mountains ahead. He turned to King, his tone urgent but measured. "Captain, we've got a potential solution. There's a labyrinth of undersea peaks about three klicks ahead. If we can thread through them, the terrain might distort their sensors enough to buy us time."

King studied the map, his eyes narrowing as he traced the proposed route. The passage was perilously narrow, the jagged peaks and sharp escarpments leaving little room for error. A single miscalculation could result in disaster.

"It's risky," King said, his tone low but steady.

Green nodded. "It is, sir. But staying here isn't an option. If we're caught in that grid, we're done."

King didn't hesitate further. "Do it. Helm, adjust course to bring us into that labyrinth. Green, you're in charge of navigation. I want constant updates on depth and clearances."

The *Oregon* banked gently, its bow turning toward the looming maze of undersea mountains. The transition was smooth, but the tension in the control room tightened like a coiled spring. Green's hands moved deftly over the controls, his voice calm as he relayed instructions to the helmsman.

"Depth to ridge line: 20 meters. Reduce speed to one-fifth. Keep us at a steady descent."

The submarine eased into the labyrinth, the towering peaks on either side casting dark shadows that seemed to press inward. The walls of the undersea mountains rose like jagged teeth, their surfaces glinting faintly in the dim light of the vessel's external lamps.

"Watch that angle," Green murmured, his eyes flicking between the map and the live feed from the sonar. "That ridge to starboard is closer than it looks. Helm, adjust two degrees port. Easy... easy..."

The *Oregon* crept forward, its movements painstakingly precise. Every groan of the hull under pressure sounded deafening in the silence, a stark reminder of the forces pressing against them.

Carter's voice cut through the tense quiet.
"Captain, the sensors are getting closer. They've already covered the northern quadrant. If we don't clear this area soon—"

"We will," King interrupted, his tone calm but resolute. "Focus on the task at hand."

Green's voice followed almost immediately. "Approaching the choke point. It's tight—only eight meters clearance on either side. Helm, take us down another five meters. Let the current guide us through."

The helmsman nodded, sweat beading on his brow as he adjusted the controls. The *Oregon* shifted slightly, the slow descent making every creak and groan of the hull feel magnified.

The choke point loomed ahead, the jagged edges of the rock walls appearing on the external cameras like the jaws of some enormous beast. The submarine moved forward, its pace agonizingly slow. In the control room, no one dared to speak. Even breathing seemed too loud.

"Depth: holding at 400 meters," Green reported, his voice steady despite the tension. "Clearance: six meters to port, seven to starboard. Helm, keep us centered."

King stood motionless, his sharp eyes scanning the displays. The moment stretched, every second feeling like an eternity. Then, with a faint ping, the *Oregon* cleared the choke point, the open expanse of the labyrinth stretching out ahead.

"Clear," Green said, exhaling for what felt like the first time in minutes. "Next waypoint: 700 meters ahead. We'll have more room to maneuver there."

King nodded. "Good work, Green. Keep us moving. Carter, status on *Sokol*?"

Carter's hands flew over her console, filtering the sonar data. "They're holding position, but the sensors are still active. If they sweep this area—"

"They won't," King interrupted, his tone leaving no room for doubt. "Stay focused. We're not out of this yet."

As the *Oregon* navigated deeper into the labyrinth, the crew's movements became a symphony of precision. Green continued to guide the submarine with a surgeon's care, his voice steady as he relayed updates. Carter's eyes remained glued to her console, tracking every blip and ripple that might indicate the *Sokol's* presence.

The undersea mountains seemed to close in around them, their jagged peaks casting long, menacing shadows. But the terrain, dangerous as it was, offered a fragile shield—a shield the crew of the *Oregon* was determined to use to their advantage.

For now, they were hidden. But the labyrinth was unforgiving, and one wrong move could spell the end.

Part 3: Shadows in the Depths

The ocean was silent, but it was a deceptive kind of silence—the kind that thrummed with unseen life and hidden danger. In the labyrinth of undersea mountains, the *Oregon* lay nestled in the shadows, its matte-black hull blending into the cold, crushing depths.

Inside, the silence was even more profound. No one spoke. Every movement was calculated, deliberate, and silent. Even the hum of the ship's systems had been muted to the bare minimum, as if the submarine itself understood the need for stealth. The crew's breaths were shallow, their focus absolute, each member keenly aware that the smallest sound could mean the difference between escape and discovery.

"Sonar waves," Carter whispered, breaking the oppressive quiet. Her voice was soft but sharp, like the edge of a knife. "They've begun scanning the terrain."

The *Sokol's* sonar pings began to echo through the hull, faint but insistent. They came in rhythmic bursts, a relentless pulse that reached out into the blackness, seeking anything that didn't belong. The sound wasn't loud, but it filled the control room like a heartbeat, each ping a reminder that the hunter was closing in.

King stepped forward, his boots making no sound on the steel floor. He stood behind Carter, his eyes locked on the display as the sonar waves rippled outward. The map on her screen showed the intricate web of the underwater mountain range, each peak and ridge now illuminated by the *Sokol's* probing signals.

"They're thorough," King murmured, his voice barely audible. "Clever, too. They're using the terrain to amplify their scans."

"They're close," Carter replied, her hands trembling slightly as she adjusted the filters on her console. "If we move, even a whisper of sound could give us away."

Green, seated at the navigation station, glanced up from his charts. "Captain, we've got an option," he said, keeping his voice low. "We can drop deeper into the trench behind us. The terrain might shield us from the direct sonar waves. But..." He hesitated.

King raised an eyebrow. "But?"

"It's the currents, sir. They're unpredictable down there. Without engines, we'll be at the mercy of the flow. If it pushes us into the rocks..." Green trailed off, the unspoken outcome hanging heavy in the air.

King considered the risk. The *Sokol* was closing in, its scans growing sharper, more methodical. Staying still was safer for now, but it left them vulnerable to the currents. Moving, however cautiously, could expose them. The choice was a grim one.

"We hold position," King decided, his tone firm. "Shut down all non-essential systems. No propulsion, no movement. We let the thermals carry us, but we stay quiet."

The order was executed with the efficiency of a well-oiled machine. The engines powered down, their low hum fading into silence. The air in the control room seemed to grow heavier as the submarine became a passive observer in the deadly game playing out around it.

Outside, the *Sokol's* sonar waves intensified, their reach growing as they combed the labyrinth. Each ping reverberated through the hull like the tolling of a distant bell, a reminder that their enemy was close—too close.

Carter's fingers hovered over her console, every muscle in her body tense. She could feel the weight of the crew's unspoken fears pressing down on her. Each blip on her screen felt like a personal threat, a challenge she couldn't afford to lose.

"They're shifting," she whispered, her voice so soft it was barely audible. "Northwest quadrant. Their sweep pattern is tightening."

King nodded, his expression unreadable. "Good. Let them think we've moved. They're looking in the wrong place. For now."

The submarine drifted, carried by the gentle push of the currents. The faint creaks and groans of the hull adjusting to the pressure seemed deafening in the stillness. Every sound felt amplified, every breath a potential betrayal.

Green kept his eyes on the navigation display, his hands gripping the edge of the console. "Current's pulling us to starboard," he said softly. "We're edging closer to the ridge. Clearance is down to seven meters."

"Monitor it," King replied. "We don't touch the controls unless we have to."

The tension in the control room was suffocating, the air heavy with anticipation. Time stretched, each second dragging out endlessly as the *Oregon* crept forward, invisible in the dark.

Suddenly, a sharper, louder ping echoed through the hull, making several crew members flinch. Carter's hands flew across her console, her breath catching as she analyzed the new signal.

"Active sonar," she whispered, her voice trembling. "They're not just scanning now—they're searching."

King's expression darkened. "How far?"

"Too close," Carter said. "Less than a kilometer."

The weight of her words sank into the room like a stone. Every eye was on the captain now, waiting for his next move. But King didn't speak immediately. He stood still, his sharp gaze fixed on the displays, his mind calculating every possibility.

"Hold your positions," he said at last, his voice calm and steady. "They're fishing. They don't know we're here, not yet. We give them nothing."

The *Oregon* hung in the water like a ghost, silent and unmoving. Outside, the sonar waves continued to ripple through the depths, relentless in their pursuit. Inside, the crew held their collective breath, their hearts pounding in their chests as they waited for the next move.

It was a deadly game of patience, and the *Oregon* was betting everything on its silence.

Part 4: The Malfunction

The *Oregon* drifted like a shadow, carried by the slow, steady currents of the abyss. Inside, the crew maintained their fragile silence, their nerves taut as sonar pings from the *Sokol* echoed faintly through the hull. Every creak, every groan of the submarine under pressure felt magnified in the oppressive stillness. And then, like a splinter in a perfect facade, something went wrong.

A sudden jolt rippled through the *Oregon*. It wasn't violent, but it was enough to make Carter's hands falter over her console and cause Green to look up sharply from his navigation station.

"What was that?" Green muttered under his breath, his eyes darting to the depth gauge.

The intercom crackled to life, breaking the tension with the urgency of Landry's voice.
"Captain, this is Landry in engineering. We've got a problem—rudder controls are glitching. The hydraulics are unstable, and we're losing response on the starboard fin."

King's eyes narrowed as he stepped toward the intercom panel. His voice was calm, but the edge of command was unmistakable. "Landry, how bad is it? Can we compensate?"

"Not for long," Landry replied, the sound of clanging tools and hurried voices echoing faintly in the background. "The system's cycling erratically. I've got my team working on it, but if it locks up completely, we're sitting ducks."

Green tightened his grip on the controls, his jaw clenched. "Captain, she's already slipping. We're drifting off course, and I'm having to fight the currents. If this gets worse—"

"Don't let it get worse," King interrupted, his tone sharp but not unkind. He turned back to the intercom. "Landry, focus everything on stabilizing that system. I don't care if it's a patch job—just keep us moving."

"Understood, Captain," Landry said. "But if this thing goes south, you'll be the first to know."

The *Oregon* groaned as Green fought to maintain their trajectory. His hands worked the controls with practiced precision, but the strain was evident. Sweat beaded on his forehead, and the muscles in his arms tensed as he countered the unpredictable shifts in the submarine's movement.

"Currents are pushing us toward the ridge," Green reported, his voice tight. "Starboard clearance is down to five meters and shrinking. If we lose the rudder entirely..."

He didn't finish the sentence, but the implication hung heavy in the air.

King's mind raced. The *Sokol's* sensors were still active, combing the labyrinth for any sign of them. Noise was their greatest enemy, but at this depth, even silence couldn't protect them from an uncontrollable drift into the jagged rocks.

"Options?" King demanded, his voice cutting through the tension.

Green's gaze flickered to the navigation map, then back to his controls. "We need to buy Landry time to fix this. If we angle her down slightly, we can let the currents pull us deeper into the trench. It'll reduce the strain on the rudder, but it's risky. Too steep, and we could nose-dive straight into the seabed."

The control room was thick with anticipation as King weighed the risks. He turned to Carter.
"Sonar update. Where's the *Sokol*?"

Carter's hands moved deftly over her console, filtering through the ambient noise. "They're holding position, but their sweep is closing in. If we shift too much, they'll pick up on it."

King nodded slowly, his expression hardening as he made his decision. "Green, take us down. Shallow angle—five degrees. Keep her steady, and watch those clearances like a hawk."

"Aye, Captain," Green said, his hands already moving to adjust the controls.

The submarine groaned again as it began its slow descent, the currents tugging at its frame. Green worked the controls with surgical precision, easing the *Oregon* into the trench. On the external cameras, the jagged walls of the undersea mountains loomed closer, their sharp edges a stark reminder of the narrow margin for error.

"Depth: 430 meters," Green reported, his voice steady despite the strain. "Clearance is tight, but holding."

In engineering, Landry barked orders to his team, the clang of tools and the hiss of escaping steam creating a chaotic symphony. "Give me more pressure on that line!" he shouted. "If we can stabilize the hydraulics, we might get control back."

"Captain," Landry's voice crackled through the intercom again, "we've got partial stabilization. Rudder's back online, but she's still shaky. Don't push her too hard."

King's lips pressed into a thin line. "Good work, Landry. Keep monitoring it. Green, how's she handling?"

Green exhaled sharply, his grip easing slightly on the controls. "Better, but she's still sluggish. We've got enough to hold our course, but I wouldn't bet on any sharp turns."

The control room fell into a tense rhythm as the *Oregon* continued its descent, now steadier but still vulnerable. Carter's eyes remained fixed on her console, tracking the faint echoes of the *Sokol's* sonar.

"They're shifting north," she reported quietly. "Sweep pattern is widening. If we stay quiet, we might just slip past them."

King allowed himself a brief nod. "Let's keep it that way. Maintain this depth and speed. Landry, keep me updated on the rudder. I want no surprises."

The crew worked in silent coordination, the weight of the moment binding them together. The *Oregon* was still in the game, but the stakes had never felt higher. One more mistake, one more failure, and they'd have no room left to maneuver.

For now, they moved forward, the shadows of the labyrinth their only shield against the relentless pursuit above.

Part 5: The Bold Idea

The *Oregon* moved cautiously, its hull creaking under the immense pressure of the depths. In the dim glow of the control room, the atmosphere hung heavy, as if the tension itself had weight. Each ping from the *Sokol* was a reminder that discovery was only a heartbeat away.

Green leaned over the navigation console, his eyes narrowing as he studied the topographical data projected before him. The jagged lines of the undersea mountains sprawled across the screen, a chaotic maze of ridges, trenches, and unseen currents. His mind raced, searching for patterns, for any anomaly he could exploit. And then, he saw it.

"Captain," Green said, his voice cutting through the low hum of the room. "I've got an idea."

King turned, his sharp gaze fixing on the young navigator. "I'm listening."

Green pointed at a section of the map, his finger tracing a narrow corridor flanked by steep ridges. "Here. This canyon isn't just a dead zone for sonar—it's a confluence point for two strong currents. If we can position ourselves just right, the turbulence will mask our presence. It'll be like finding a hiding spot in the eye of a storm."

The crew exchanged uncertain glances. Carter, still monitoring the sonar, looked up from her console. "That's risky. If we miscalculate the entry point or the currents shift, we could get pulled into the rocks. And what happens if *Sokol* decides to follow the turbulence?"

"They won't," Green replied confidently. "Active sonar struggles with chaotic environments like this. Their readings will be too noisy to pinpoint us."

King studied the map, his expression unreadable. The proposed maneuver was audacious, the kind of gamble that could save them—or doom them. He turned back to Green.
"What kind of coordination are we talking about? Can we execute this without lighting up like a Christmas tree?"

Green nodded, though his tone was cautious. "It'll be tight. We'll need precise control of the rudder and speed to slip into the current's flow. Landry's team will have to monitor the hydraulics like hawks. And Carter—" He glanced at her. "You'll need to track *Sokol's* position in real time. If they change course, we'll have to adapt instantly."

The intercom crackled to life as Landry's voice filled the room. "Captain, I hope you're not about to ask for fancy steering. We're barely holding this system together."

"Landry," King replied, a faint edge of humor in his tone, "when have I ever asked you for something easy?"

"Fair point," Landry muttered, the clanging of tools audible in the background. "Just keep her steady, and we'll make it work. But if this rudder blows, you're on your own."

"Noted," King said dryly before turning to the crew. "You heard him. This is going to be surgical. Green, you have the helm. Carter, keep us informed. Everyone else—stay sharp."

The *Oregon* adjusted its course, edging toward the turbulent zone. The submarine crept forward with painstaking precision, every movement calculated. Green's hands were steady on the controls, his eyes darting between the map and the external cameras. The faint shimmer of the currents ahead created ghostly patterns in the water, a visual reminder of the forces they were about to face.

"Approaching the convergence point," Green reported. "Speed: one-fifth. Clearance: four meters port, three starboard."

"Hold steady," King ordered, his voice calm but firm.

In the sonar station, Carter's fingers flew over her console as she filtered through the chaotic echoes. Her heart pounded as she tracked *Sokol's* position. Suddenly, the faint pings began to fade.

"They're shifting north," she said, her voice tinged with cautious optimism. "Their sweep is weakening. They're recalibrating—probably trying to make sense of the noise."

King nodded. "That gives us a window. Let's use it."

The *Oregon* slipped into the currents, the submarine jolting slightly as the turbulence wrapped around it. Green adjusted the controls, his movements precise as he aligned the vessel with the flow. The rushing water created a protective shield of sound, a natural camouflage against the *Sokol's* relentless scans.

"Depth holding at 450 meters," Green reported, his voice steady despite the strain. "Currents are stabilizing. We're in the pocket."

Landry's voice crackled over the intercom. "Hydraulics are holding—for now. Don't push her too hard."

For a moment, the control room was filled with quiet relief. The *Oregon* was hidden, nestled in the chaos of the currents. Carter continued to monitor the *Sokol*, her focus unbroken.

"They're not following," she confirmed after a tense minute. "We're clear—for now."

King allowed himself a brief exhale. "Good work, everyone. Stay alert. We're not out of the woods yet."

The submarine floated in the eye of the storm, its crew finally daring to hope. The tension had not vanished, but it had shifted, replaced by a flicker of confidence in their ability to outmaneuver their pursuers. For the first time since the chase began, they had found a momentary sanctuary—and the ingenuity of their navigator had made it possible.

Part 6: The Breakthrough

The *Oregon* lay suspended in the embrace of the undersea currents, its sleek frame vibrating subtly as the rushing water formed a natural veil around it. In the control room, every member of the crew was on edge, their movements careful and precise. The gamble Green had proposed was about to be tested, and there was no room for error.

"Entering the vortex zone," Green reported, his voice steady but clipped. His hands gripped the controls with precision, his eyes darting between the navigation map and the live feed from the external cameras.

The display showed a mesmerizing spectacle outside the submarine. The swirling currents twisted and danced like ethereal ribbons in the dim blue light, creating an otherworldly kaleidoscope of motion. The water churned with powerful turbulence, forming whorls and eddies that obscured the *Oregon's* presence. It was both beautiful and perilous—a sanctuary for the daring, a deathtrap for the careless.

Landry's voice crackled through the intercom, cutting through the tense quiet.
"Hydraulics are holding, but don't push her too hard. If we get caught in the wrong flow, I'm not sure this patch job will keep us intact."

King pressed the intercom button. "We'll keep her steady, Landry. Just be ready for anything."

The captain turned his attention to Green, who was locked in concentration.
"Talk to me, Green. How's she handling?"

"Currents are strong, but we're in control," Green replied, his tone focused. "Adjusting rudder five degrees port to align with the vortex flow. Speed: one-sixth. This is the sweet spot. If we push any faster, we'll lose stability."

King gave a sharp nod. "Good. Keep her in the flow. Carter, where's the *Sokol*?"

Carter's hands moved deftly over her console as she filtered through the cacophony of sonar signals.
"They're holding position for now, but their sensors are still sweeping. The turbulence is interfering—it's working." She paused, her brow furrowing. "Wait. They're shifting course… heading north. I think they're losing us."

A ripple of relief swept through the control room, though no one dared to exhale fully. The crew knew better than to celebrate prematurely. Green tightened his grip on the controls as the submarine eased deeper into the vortex. The currents grew wilder, the water around them a swirling tempest of sound and motion.

"Depth: 480 meters," Green called out. "Clearance is holding. The turbulence is masking most of our signature."

The external cameras captured the chaotic beauty of the undersea maelstrom. Shimmering particles of sediment danced in the currents, their paths erratic and hypnotic. The submarine's lights cast faint halos, illuminating jagged ridges and deep, shadowed crevices that loomed like sleeping giants.

"Steady as she goes," King said, his voice calm but commanding. "This is where we earn our keep."

Landry's voice broke through again, a mix of tension and gruff humor. "Captain, I hope you've got Green on a tight leash. These hydraulics weren't built for ballet."

King smirked faintly. "Don't worry, Landry. Green's not dancing—he's performing surgery."

"That's supposed to make me feel better?" Landry grumbled, though the faint hint of a chuckle softened his words.

As the *Oregon* pressed further into the vortex, the currents seemed to cradle the submarine, guiding it along their natural flow. The chaotic noise of the maelstrom drowned out the faint hum of the vessel's systems, rendering it almost invisible to the *Sokol's* sensors.

Carter's voice, sharp and focused, cut through the quiet.
"*Sokol's* sonar sweeps are fading. Their course is changing—northwest. They've lost us."

A palpable wave of relief washed over the control room. Green eased back on the controls, his shoulders relaxing slightly for the first time in hours.

"We're clear—for now," Carter added, her tone cautious.

King allowed himself a brief moment of satisfaction, though his expression remained steely. "Good work, everyone. But don't let your guard down. Green, maintain our position until we're sure they're out of range. Carter, keep tracking them."

The *Oregon* hung silently in the vortex, its crew finally daring to hope. Outside, the swirling currents continued their chaotic dance, a natural shield that had given them a fragile reprieve. The control room was quieter now, but the tension lingered, tempered by the knowledge that their safety was only temporary.

King stood at the center of it all, his sharp gaze sweeping over his team. They were exhausted but resolute, their unity forged in the crucible of survival.

"Make no mistake," he said, his voice low but firm. "We've bought ourselves time, but this isn't over. The *Sokol* will regroup, and when they do, we'll need to be ready."

The crew nodded, their determination unshaken. For now, the *Oregon* was safe, hidden in the chaos of the undersea vortex. It was a victory, but a fleeting one—and they all knew it.

Part 7: Reflections and Resolve

The *Oregon* floated silently in the dim depths, a shadow among shadows. In the control room, the tension that had gripped the crew for hours finally began to loosen. The harsh fluorescent lights cast a stark glow on weary faces, but there was a quiet pride in their exhaustion. They had survived—not by luck, but through skill, ingenuity, and teamwork.

Captain King stood at the center of it all, his posture steady, his sharp eyes scanning the room. He saw it in their faces: the fatigue, the unspoken fear of how close they had come to disaster, but also the flicker of confidence. This crew had been tested, and they had proven themselves.

"Ladies and gentlemen," King began, his voice calm yet commanding, "what we just pulled off was nothing short of extraordinary. We faced a superior hunter on its own turf, and we came out unscathed. That doesn't happen by accident. It happens because of each and every one of you."

He looked first to Carter, who was still seated at her sonar console, her hands resting lightly on the edges as if bracing for another wave of tension.
"Carter," King said, his tone softening slightly, "you tracked that Russian boat with a precision that would make any sonar operator proud. Without your vigilance, we wouldn't be here right now."

Carter nodded, a faint smile tugging at the corners of her lips. "Just doing my job, sir."

King's gaze shifted to Green, who was standing by the navigation station, his uniform slightly rumpled but his posture resolute.
"And Green," King continued, "your plan was bold, but it worked. You

took a calculated risk, and you executed it flawlessly. This crew owes you their lives."

Green, always modest, simply inclined his head. "Wouldn't have meant much without the team to back me up, sir."

The intercom crackled as Landry's gruff voice filled the room. "And don't forget the folks down here in engineering, Captain," he said. "We kept this bird flying—or, well, floating—while you were up there making all the big decisions."

A ripple of quiet laughter spread through the control room, easing the tension further. King allowed himself a small smile.
"Landry, I couldn't forget you if I tried. Your team did an exceptional job. We'll need to debrief on those hydraulics, though. I don't want to see another failure like that."

"Trust me, neither do I," Landry replied, a hint of humor masking his fatigue. "We'll overhaul the whole system if we have to."

As the laughter faded, a solemnity settled over the room. The crew knew how close they had been to catastrophe. Carter broke the silence, her voice quieter than usual.
"Captain... we were seconds away from losing control out there. If those currents had shifted even a little, or if the *Sokol* had recalibrated faster..."

She didn't finish, but she didn't need to. The weight of her words hung in the air, a reminder of how fragile their survival had been.

King nodded slowly, his expression serious. "You're right, Carter. This mission has tested us in ways we couldn't have anticipated. But we didn't falter. We adapted. We persevered. That's what makes us who we are."

Green leaned against the edge of his station, his voice thoughtful. "Still, we can't ignore the lessons here. We need to revisit our protocols—both navigation and engineering. We need to be faster, sharper, more prepared."

"Agreed," King said firmly. "Landry, coordinate with Green and Carter. I want a full systems review. We'll identify every weak point and address it. No exceptions."

"Yes, sir," Landry replied. "But maybe let me sleep first?"

Another chuckle rippled through the crew, lighter this time, as the tension began to dissolve entirely.

King straightened, his voice steady and confident. "We've been through hell today, but we're still here. That's a testament to this crew—to your skills, your discipline, and your resilience. The ocean is vast, and the enemy is relentless, but I wouldn't trade this team for anything."

The crew stood a little taller at his words, their pride evident despite their exhaustion. In that moment, they weren't just individuals working together; they were a unit, a family bound by shared trials and triumphs.

As the crew began to disperse to their stations, Carter lingered at her console. Her sharp eyes scanned the sonar display, now quiet except for the faint background hum of the ocean.

"They're gone for now," she murmured, almost to herself.

King, still nearby, overheard her and placed a hand on the back of her chair. "For now," he agreed. "But they'll be back. And so will we. Ready and waiting."

The *Oregon* resumed its slow, steady journey through the deep. The shadows of the undersea mountains loomed around them, a reminder of the dangers that still lay ahead. But for the first time in hours, the crew moved with a renewed sense of purpose.

The silence of the ocean was no longer oppressive; it was a challenge, one they were ready to face. The *Oregon* pressed forward, still hidden in the depths but armed with the confidence that they could outmaneuver anything—or anyone—that came their way.

A hint of something larger loomed on the horizon, an unseen threat waiting beyond the shadows. But for now, the *Oregon* sailed on, stronger and more united than ever.

Part 1: Static in the Air

The faint hum of the radio console filled the otherwise silent communication bay, a steady background noise that typically blended into the rhythm of the submarine's daily operations. But to Lieutenant Carter, something was off. Her sharp eyes flickered over the spectrum analyzer, where a series of irregular spikes caught her attention. She leaned forward, her brow furrowing as she adjusted the dials, amplifying the signal.

At first, it was subtle—barely distinguishable from the usual oceanic interference. But as she fine-tuned the settings, the pattern became clearer. Short bursts of transmission, timed irregularly, threaded through the ambient noise like whispers in the dark.

"This isn't right," she murmured to herself, her fingers dancing over the controls. The transmission wasn't part of their encrypted communications. It wasn't a distress signal or a routine check-in. It was… something else.

Her mind raced as she cross-referenced the logs, pulling up timestamps and correlating the signals with recent activity aboard the *Oregon*. The data was sparse, but the timing didn't align with any official operations.

She bit her lip, her thoughts spiraling. Could this be equipment malfunction? Unlikely—the submarine's systems were checked meticulously. Random noise? No, the pattern was too deliberate. Then a chilling thought surfaced, unbidden: *What if it's someone on board?*

Her stomach tightened. The possibility was absurd, wasn't it? The crew of the *Oregon* was a tightly-knit group of professionals, each selected for their skill and loyalty. And yet, the evidence on her screen suggested something insidious—an anomaly that demanded answers.

Carter pushed back from the console and stood, her hands trembling slightly. She clenched them into fists to steady herself. The dim lighting of the room cast long shadows across the walls, amplifying the sense of isolation. She needed to act, but how?

Keep calm, Carter, she thought, taking a deep breath. *This could be nothing. But if it's not...*

She made her way to the control room, her boots echoing softly against the steel floor. Each step felt heavier than the last, weighed down by the implications of what she'd found. By the time she reached Captain King's station, her resolve was steel, even if her nerves were frayed.

"Captain," she began, her voice steady despite the storm brewing inside her. "I've picked up something unusual in the radio transmissions. Irregular bursts, short in duration. They don't match any of our operational protocols."

King turned to face her, his sharp gaze narrowing. "Could it be interference? Oceanic noise?"

Carter shook her head. "No, sir. The pattern is too deliberate. I've analyzed the logs—it doesn't correlate with anything we've transmitted or received. It's... external, but localized." She hesitated. "Possibly originating from within the submarine."

King's expression darkened, his jaw tightening. He was silent for a moment, the weight of her words sinking in. When he finally spoke, his tone was measured, but there was an edge to it. "Does anyone else know about this?"

"No, sir," Carter replied. "I wanted to bring it directly to you."

"Good," he said, his voice firm. "And it stays that way. Whatever this is, we can't afford a panic. Continue monitoring the signals, but keep it discreet. Report anything unusual directly to me—and only to me."

Carter nodded, but the unease gnawed at her. She trusted King implicitly; his leadership had guided them through countless dangers. But this was different. This was *inside*.

As she returned to her station, her thoughts spiraled further. She replayed the logs in her mind, scrutinizing every detail. Who could possibly be transmitting? And why?

The shadows in the room felt deeper now, the hum of the radio more ominous. Carter's hands hovered over the controls, her focus razor-sharp. She had a mission within a mission now—to uncover the truth. And the stakes were higher than ever.

If there is a traitor among us, she thought, her pulse quickening, *I will find them. Before they find us.*

The screen before her flickered faintly, the irregular spikes still visible. It was a small anomaly, barely noticeable in the grand scheme of the *Oregon's* operation. But to Carter, it felt like the opening note of a dangerous symphony—one that could unravel everything.

Part 2: The Hidden Danger

The hum of the *Oregon's* systems blended seamlessly with the faint creaks of the submarine as it adjusted to the pressure of the deep. In the control room, Captain King's sharp gaze swept over the crew. Each movement, each murmur seemed magnified under the weight of his silent scrutiny. Whatever was happening on his boat, it had to be stopped before it escalated.

King leaned closer to Green and Carter, his voice low but commanding. "We need to narrow this down. Someone on this sub has access to the communications systems. Start with the logs—who's been near the radio equipment, who's had access to sensitive areas. I don't care how small the overlap is; I want names."

Green nodded, his jaw set with determination. "On it, Captain."

Carter hesitated, her mind already racing through the possibilities. "And the transmission logs—if there's a pattern, it might match shifts or specific personnel movements. I'll cross-reference everything."

King's eyes softened slightly as he met her gaze. "Good. But remember, this stays between us for now. If word gets out that we're investigating, it could push the traitor to act recklessly. Or worse."

In the bowels of the submarine, Landry's engineering team worked in near silence. The normally gruff and boisterous chief was unusually focused, his brow furrowed as he inspected the guts of the communication system. Each wire, each circuit was examined with meticulous care, but nothing seemed out of place.

"Damn it," Landry muttered, wiping his hands on his oil-streaked rag. "Everything's clean. If someone's tampered with this system, they're a ghost."

One of his technicians hesitated before speaking. "Could it be an external fault? Maybe something we picked up from the environment?"

Landry shot him a sharp look. "We're not chasing phantoms. If there's a problem, it's here. And it's human."

Back in the communications bay, Carter poured over the data. The irregular signals she'd identified earlier replayed in her mind as she scrutinized the logs. Her fingers flew over the keyboard, matching timestamps with crew movement records, searching for any overlap that could explain the mysterious transmissions. And then, there it was—a pattern.

Her eyes narrowed as she traced the movements of one crew member. Each time the signal had appeared, this individual had been unaccounted for. It wasn't proof, but it was enough to send a chill down her spine.

Carter's thoughts churned as she considered the implications. Could it be a coincidence? Or was she staring at the breadcrumbs of a traitor's trail?

She found King in the control room, his presence a steady anchor in the storm of her thoughts. Approaching him quietly, she handed him her tablet.
"I found something," she said, her voice barely above a whisper.

King scanned the data, his face unreadable. "Unaccounted movements. Same time as the transmissions."

Carter nodded. "It's circumstantial, but it's something. The same crew member wasn't on station for the last three signals. It's too consistent to ignore."

King's jaw tightened as he handed back the tablet. "Good work. But it's not enough. Keep watching. We need something concrete before we make a move."

The weight of suspicion hung heavy in the air as Carter returned to her station. She tried to focus, but the thought gnawed at her: someone she worked with, someone she trusted, could be betraying them all. Each face she passed in the narrow corridors seemed shadowed with potential guilt.

Meanwhile, Green sifted through personnel records, his mind as sharp as his resolve. Every name, every duty roster, every deviation from protocol was examined under his critical eye. He felt the weight of King's directive pressing on him—this wasn't just about identifying a suspect; it was about protecting the integrity of the *Oregon*.

Hours later, Landry radioed in from engineering.
"Captain, I've checked every system down here. If someone's using our equipment to transmit, they're damn good at covering their tracks. No tampering, no reroutes—nothing."

King's voice was calm but firm. "Keep looking, Landry. If they've hidden their trail this well, it means they're skilled—and dangerous."

As the day stretched into the tense quiet of evening, Carter's screen flickered with a new alert. Her heart leapt into her throat as she recognized the pattern—a fresh transmission. She traced it immediately, and her stomach dropped. The timing matched perfectly with another unexplained absence.

Her fingers hesitated over the keyboard. This wasn't just a coincidence anymore. The pieces were coming together, but the picture they formed was far darker than she had anticipated.

She reached for the intercom but stopped herself. This needed to go directly to King, and no one else. Rising from her seat, she moved swiftly down the corridor, her mind racing with the implications. The *Oregon* wasn't just battling threats from the depths—it was fighting something far more insidious within.

Part 3: Shadows of Suspicion

The *Oregon* felt heavier than ever, though it wasn't the crushing weight of the ocean depths pressing against the hull. It was the atmosphere within—the crackling tension that hung in the air, thick and suffocating. The faint whispers of suspicion had spread like an insidious fog, curling through the submarine's narrow corridors, seeping into every crevice of the crew's collective psyche.

It began with a slip—a careless remark made by an officer who should have known better. In the mess hall, over a hastily eaten meal, the words had been murmured in frustration, intended for no one but the tablemate seated across. But the walls of the *Oregon* had ears.

"There's something happening with the comms," the officer had said, his tone edged with uncertainty. "Carter and the captain are working on it. Might be sabotage."

By the time the rumor reached the lower decks, it had metastasized into something far more dangerous.

The crew began eyeing each other with quiet suspicion. Once-fluid conversations were now fragmented, marked by hesitations and unspoken thoughts. Friendships forged through shared trials and sleepless nights became brittle under the strain of mistrust. Every accidental glance became a potential accusation, every pause in duty a sign of guilt.

"I saw Daniels near the radio room last night," someone whispered.

"Do you think it's Jenkins? He's been acting strange lately."

"What about Carter herself? She's the one who found it. What if she's covering her tracks?"

In the torpedo bay, the simmering tension finally boiled over. Mathews, a hot-tempered crewman with a reputation for speaking his mind, slammed his fist onto the steel workbench, the clang echoing through the small, cramped space. His anger, unchecked, spilled out in a sharp accusation.

"Enough of this sneaking around, Collins!" he snapped, his voice cutting through the tense silence. "You think no one notices? You're always slipping off during shifts. Where the hell do you go?"

Collins froze, his expression morphing from shock to indignation. "What the hell are you talking about?" he fired back. "I do my job. Maybe you should stop worrying about me and focus on your own damn tasks."

Mathews took a step closer, his fists clenched. "Don't play innocent. You've been disappearing, and now we've got these mysterious transmissions. Coincidence? I don't think so."

Collins' face darkened with anger. "You're insane. If anyone's got something to hide, it's you! Always pretending to be Mr. Perfect. Maybe you're trying to shift the blame."

The other crew members in the bay stood frozen, their eyes darting between the two men. The tension was palpable, like the charged air before a storm. It was clear that neither man would back down.

The sound of boots striking steel cut through the rising noise. Captain King's arrival was swift and authoritative, his mere presence enough to silence the escalating argument. He didn't need to shout; his tone was colder than the deep waters outside.

"What is going on here?" King demanded, his voice a low growl that carried the weight of absolute command.

Mathews took a step back, the fire in his expression extinguished. "Just... a misunderstanding, Captain."

"A misunderstanding?" King's piercing gaze swept over the two men, then the rest of the room. "Let me make something perfectly clear. This submarine operates on discipline and trust. Lose either, and we're dead before the enemy even has a chance to act."

He turned his attention back to Mathews. "Accusations without proof are more dangerous than any weapon. If you can't substantiate your claims, keep your mouth shut. Understood?"

"Yes, sir," Mathews muttered, his bravado reduced to ashes.

King shifted his focus to Collins, his tone no less sharp. "And you—if there's any truth to what's been said, you'd better bring it to me. But until then, you'll carry out your duties without distraction. Is that clear?"

Collins' jaw tightened, but he nodded. "Crystal clear, Captain."

King took a moment to survey the room, his icy gaze freezing everyone in place. "This is your warning. We don't have the luxury of turning on each other. Whoever is responsible for these transmissions, I will find them. And if any of you think you can take matters into your own hands, think again."

He left the room in heavy silence, his words hanging over the crew like a storm cloud.

Back in the control room, King's expression was grim as he leaned over the console, his thoughts a storm of their own. Carter approached cautiously, her worry evident.

"I heard what happened in the torpedo bay," she said quietly. "It's spreading faster than we expected."

King exhaled sharply, his frustration bleeding through the otherwise calm exterior. "The crew is cracking under the pressure. If we don't find the source of these transmissions soon, they'll tear themselves apart before the enemy even has a chance."

Carter hesitated, then said, "I'll keep digging. I'm getting closer to isolating the signal. If there's a pattern, I'll find it."

King nodded, his voice softer. "I trust you, Carter. But be careful. Whatever's behind this isn't just about sabotage—it's deliberate. And whoever's responsible knows what they're doing."

That evening, the submarine was quieter than usual, but it wasn't the quiet of rest. It was the silence of a crew wrestling with doubt, with fear, with the shadows of suspicion that lingered in every corner. Conversations were stilted, and even the familiar hum of the submarine's systems felt colder, more mechanical.

In the dim corridors of the *Oregon*, trust was the first casualty, and the true enemy still lurked unseen.

Part 4: Observation

The dim glow of the control room lights painted sharp contrasts on Carter's face as she worked, her fingers deftly connecting wires to a compact tracking module. Next to her, Green leaned over a schematic of the *Oregon's* communication network, his brow furrowed in concentration.

"This isn't just about pinpointing a signal," Carter murmured, her voice low, more to herself than anyone else. "We need to catch them in the act."

Green nodded, tracing a cable route on the map. "If they've been smart enough to avoid detection so far, they're not going to make it easy. Every step has to be precise."

In the engineering bay, Landry studied the guts of one of the submarine's auxiliary radio systems, his sleeves rolled up and a faint scowl etched across his face. The hum of machinery filled the space, but his focus was on the tangle of wires and circuits in front of him.

"Come on, where are you hiding?" he muttered, his hands methodically testing connections and inspecting components.

Then he saw it—a tiny modification, so subtle it would have gone unnoticed during routine maintenance. It was a bypass circuit, expertly integrated, diverting a fraction of the outgoing signal.

"Well, I'll be damned," Landry breathed. He pressed the intercom button. "Captain, I've found something. Secondary comm system, portside. There's a modification here—clean work, but definitely not standard. No way this was done by accident."

In the briefing room, King studied the evidence laid before him. Carter's tracking devices, Green's schematics, and Landry's discovery formed a chilling picture. Someone aboard the *Oregon* had not only gained unauthorized access to the communication systems but had also expertly masked their activities.

King's jaw tightened as he formulated a plan. "We're not dealing with an amateur," he said, his tone sharp. "If we confront them outright, they'll either deny it or go dark. We need to draw them out, force them to act."

He turned to Carter and Green. "I want to simulate a high-priority transmission—something too tempting for them to ignore. Make it look urgent but vague enough to spark curiosity."

Carter exchanged a glance with Green. "And if they bite?" she asked.

"They'll try to intercept or piggyback on the signal," King replied. "And when they do, we'll know exactly who and where they are."

As the plan took shape, the tension aboard the *Oregon* grew palpable. The crew sensed the shift in atmosphere, though the details of the operation were kept tightly controlled. Whispers circulated among the ranks, speculation filling the gaps left by silence.

"What's going on?" a young ensign whispered to a fellow crew member. "Everyone's acting like we're about to hit a minefield."

"Probably just another drill," came the reply, though the uncertainty in their voice betrayed their unease.

In the control room, Carter and Green finalized the preparations. Carter carefully programmed the false transmission, her fingers steady despite the weight of the moment. Green monitored the network, his eyes scanning for any anomalies.

"Are we ready?" King asked, stepping into the room.

"Ready as we'll ever be," Carter replied, her tone calm but resolute.

King glanced at his officers. "Remember, no one outside this room knows the full extent of what we're doing. If anyone asks, it's a standard communications test. We can't risk tipping off whoever's behind this."

The submarine fell into a tense quiet as the operation began. Carter activated the transmission, sending the carefully crafted signal into the ether. It was designed to appear critical but cryptic, enough to tempt the saboteur without revealing the ruse.

Time seemed to stretch as the crew carried out their duties, oblivious to the trap being laid. In the control room, Carter's eyes remained fixed on her screen, watching for the faintest blip that would indicate someone was trying to access the system.

Next to her, Green monitored the network's activity, his muscles taut with anticipation. "If they make a move, we'll see it," he said quietly, more to reassure himself than anyone else.

King stood behind them, his presence steady and unyielding. His gaze was fixed on the silent ocean beyond the thick glass of the control room, but his mind was on the unseen enemy within.

"Let's see if they take the bait," he murmured.

The minutes dragged on, each one heavier than the last. The hum of the submarine's systems and the faint creak of the hull under pressure were the only sounds in the control room. The tension was suffocating, a silent storm brewing just beneath the surface.

And then, Carter's screen flickered. A spike in the signal.

"Captain," she said, her voice cutting through the quiet like a blade. "We've got something."

King leaned forward, his eyes narrowing. "Track it. Now."

Carter's hands flew across the keyboard as she triangulated the source. Green adjusted the network view, isolating the anomaly.

"It's coming from the lower decks," Carter reported, her tone urgent. "They're piggybacking off the transmission."

King's expression hardened. "We've got them."

The silent storm broke, and the hunt within the *Oregon* had truly begun.

Part 5: Caught in the Net

The tension aboard the *Oregon* had reached a breaking point. Every creak of the hull, every whispered word in the narrow corridors felt magnified, echoing through the minds of the crew. But in the control room, the air was razor-sharp, brimming with anticipation. The trap was set, and now it was only a matter of time before it snapped shut.

Carter sat at her console, her fingers poised above the keyboard, her gaze locked on the screens in front of her. Each flicker of light on the monitors felt like a heartbeat, pulsing with the unspoken urgency that filled the room.

"Signal is live," Carter announced, her voice steady despite the weight of the moment. She activated the simulated transmission, a carefully constructed message designed to appear critical—a supposed emergency course adjustment, dressed in just enough technical jargon to pique curiosity.

The message began to propagate, weaving its way through the *Oregon*'s communication systems. Green, stationed in the radio room, kept his eyes on the equipment, watching for any sign of interference. The dim red lighting in the cramped space cast shadows that danced across the walls, adding an almost spectral quality to the scene.

It didn't take long.

"Carter," Green's voice crackled over the comms, low but urgent. "We've got activity on the line. Someone's piggybacking on the signal."

In the control room, Carter's fingers flew over the keyboard, isolating the anomaly and triangulating its source. Her eyes narrowed as she tracked the unauthorized access point.

"Lower deck, engineering corridor," she reported. "It's coming from one of the auxiliary terminals."

King, standing behind her, leaned forward, his voice calm but laced with iron resolve. "Green, eyes open. We're closing in."

In the radio room, Green felt the tension like a physical weight. The faint hum of the equipment was suddenly drowned out by the sound of footsteps—soft, deliberate, heading toward the exit. He glanced up and caught a glimpse of movement: a figure trying to slip away, their shadow stretching long against the walls.

"Got you," Green muttered under his breath.

He moved swiftly, his boots barely making a sound on the steel floor. Blocking the doorway, he straightened to his full height, his voice firm but quiet. "Where do you think you're going?"

The figure froze. It was an engineer, a quiet and unassuming member of the crew who had always blended into the background. His face was pale, his eyes darting nervously as if searching for an escape route.

"I—uh, just checking the systems," the engineer stammered, his voice wavering. "Routine maintenance."

"Funny," Green replied, his tone sharp. "Routine maintenance doesn't usually involve unauthorized access to comm systems."

King and a small team arrived moments later, their presence filling the narrow corridor with an air of command. The engineer's shoulders slumped as he realized there was no way out. Carter joined them, her tablet in hand, displaying the incriminating evidence.

"This terminal," she said, pointing to the screen. "It matches the location of the unauthorized access. He was sending the signal."

The engineer's eyes darted from the screen to King, then to the others. Beads of sweat formed on his brow as he opened his mouth to speak but then closed it, lips pressed into a thin line.

King stepped forward, his gaze unyielding. "You've been caught red-handed. I suggest you start talking. Who are you working with? What have you been sending?"

The engineer shook his head, his jaw tightening. "I—I can't..." His voice broke off, barely a whisper.

"You can't, or you won't?" King's voice cut through the silence like a blade.

The engineer didn't respond. The defiance—or perhaps fear—in his eyes was clear.

The tension in the corridor was suffocating, every crew member present holding their breath. Green crossed his arms, his expression dark. "You're putting the entire boat at risk. You realize that, don't you?"

Still, the engineer said nothing. Carter exchanged a look with King, her frustration evident. "Captain, if he doesn't cooperate, we can't rule out the possibility that he's not working alone."

King nodded slowly, his mind working through the layers of complexity this revelation had added. "Secure him. Lock down this section of the deck and sweep for any additional devices. We're not taking any chances."

Two crew members stepped forward to escort the engineer away. He didn't resist, though his silence spoke volumes, leaving an unsettling impression on everyone who watched him disappear down the corridor.

Back in the control room, King addressed his senior officers, his voice steady but tinged with the weight of the situation. "We've made progress, but this isn't over. We don't know how much information he's already sent—or who else might be involved. From this moment on, no one operates outside their assigned tasks. Every movement, every action is logged and accounted for. Understood?"

"Yes, sir," came the unified response.

As Carter returned to her station, she felt a mix of relief and unease. They had caught someone, but the unanswered questions hung heavy in the air. Was this engineer truly the only one? Or was he just a piece of a larger puzzle?

The faint hum of the systems filled the control room once more, but it no longer felt routine. Every sound, every flicker of light on the monitors seemed to carry the weight of hidden intentions. Somewhere in the dark, the *Oregon*'s true enemy might still be lurking. And the crew knew they were far from safe.

Part 6: Internal Investigation

The interrogation room was a small, unadorned space deep within the *Oregon*'s labyrinthine interior. The hum of the submarine's systems resonated faintly through the walls, a constant reminder of the hostile environment pressing against the vessel. In the center of the room, under the sharp beam of a single overhead light, the detained engineer sat stiffly, his hands clasped tightly in his lap. Sweat glistened on his forehead, but his face was a mask of defiance—though it cracked slightly whenever his eyes flicked to the man standing before him.

Captain King's presence filled the room. He stood with his arms crossed, his piercing gaze fixed on the engineer, his silence more unnerving than any raised voice could have been. When King finally spoke, his voice was calm, deliberate, and sharper than the knife's edge.

"You've put this entire vessel in danger," King began, his words slicing through the tension. "You've jeopardized the lives of every man and woman aboard. The only question now is why."

The engineer hesitated, his mouth opening and closing as if the words he wanted to say were too heavy to lift. Finally, his shoulders sagged, and the first crack in his armor appeared.

"They... they forced me," he muttered, barely above a whisper.

King's brow furrowed. "Who forced you?"

The engineer licked his lips nervously. "The Soviets. I didn't have a choice. They—they know about my family. They said if I didn't cooperate, they'd..." His voice faltered, and he lowered his gaze to the table, unable to finish the sentence.

King's jaw tightened, but his voice remained steady. "How long has this been going on? What have you given them?"

The engineer shook his head, his hands gripping the edge of the table as though it might anchor him against the weight of his guilt. "It started before this mission. They contacted me through... someone. I don't even know his name. At first, it was just small things—insignificant details, nothing that could harm anyone. But then they wanted more. They always want more."

King leaned forward, his tone hardening. "And the signals? What were you transmitting from this boat?"

"Position updates," the engineer admitted. "Routine operations, course adjustments. Nothing classified—at least, nothing I thought could be used against us."

King's eyes narrowed. "You're telling me they went to all this trouble for mundane updates? Do you think I'm that naive?"

The engineer looked up, his face pale, his eyes wide with desperation. "I swear, that's all I sent! I didn't want to do any of it, but they—they had me cornered."

Meanwhile, Carter and Landry were deep in the bowels of the submarine, conducting a painstaking search of the communication systems. The modified terminal was only the tip of the iceberg, and they knew it. With every cable inspected, every circuit tested, the pieces of the puzzle became clearer.

"Look at this," Carter said, crouching beside an auxiliary panel. She pointed to a faint, almost imperceptible splice in one of the data lines. "This wasn't part of the original wiring. It's been rerouted."

Landry leaned in, his eyes narrowing as he traced the connection. "Whoever did this knew exactly what they were doing. It's clean work—professional. This wasn't some amateur job."

Carter nodded grimly. "It matches what we found on the other terminal. They were running parallel systems, piggybacking on the main network without tripping any alarms."

Landry let out a low whistle. "They've been busy."

Back in the control room, Green stood by the navigation console, his mind racing. Something about the engineer's story didn't sit right with him. If the Soviets had gone to such lengths to plant someone on the *Oregon*, why rely on a single operative? The complexity of the modifications, the precision of the transmissions—it felt too sophisticated for one man to manage alone.

"I don't like it," Green muttered, half to himself.

Carter glanced up from her station. "What?"

"The engineer," Green said, his voice thoughtful. "He's telling us what we want to hear, but I don't think he's working alone. It's too big for one person."

Carter frowned. "Do you have proof?"

"Not yet," Green admitted. "But I'll find it."

By the time King reconvened with his senior officers, the mood aboard the submarine had grown heavier. The crew was on edge, their whispers of suspicion now underpinned by a tangible sense of unease. King knew he had to act decisively to maintain control, but he also understood the fine line he was walking. Too much transparency, and the crew could descend into paranoia. Too little, and the fractures in their unity would deepen.

"Here's how we proceed," King said, his tone firm as he addressed his team. "The crew needs to know there's a threat aboard. They deserve to be prepared. But we don't give them details. The fewer people who know the full extent of what we're dealing with, the better."

Carter raised an eyebrow. "You think they can handle it?"

"They don't have a choice," King replied. "None of us do."

Later that evening, King addressed the crew in the mess hall. His voice carried a weight that silenced the quiet murmurs and drew every eye to him.

"Ladies and gentlemen," he began, "we've identified an internal security issue. Measures are being taken to address it, but I need each of you to remain focused on your duties. Trust in your chain of command, and trust in each other. That's the only way we get through this."

The crew nodded, their expressions a mix of determination and unease. King held their gaze a moment longer before dismissing them, leaving the room in a somber silence.

As the *Oregon* continued its silent course through the depths, the investigation pressed on. The shadows of suspicion still lingered, and though one traitor had been caught, the question remained: was he the only one? Or was the true enemy still watching, biding their time, waiting for the next move?

The hunt was far from over.

Part 7: Unity or Chaos

The mess hall was silent, save for the faint hum of the *Oregon's* systems reverberating through the steel walls. The entire crew had gathered, their faces a mix of tension, doubt, and guarded curiosity. They had all heard whispers of the incident. Something had gone wrong—terribly wrong— and now their captain stood before them, a commanding presence against the backdrop of the submarine's stark interior.

Captain King took a slow breath, letting his gaze sweep over the room. He could feel their unease, the ripple of doubt threatening to destabilize the delicate balance that kept the *Oregon* running. He had faced storms at sea, but this storm—within the hearts and minds of his crew—was unlike any other.

"When we set out on this mission," King began, his voice steady but carrying an edge, "each of you knew the risks. You knew the challenges we would face. And you knew that our success would depend on one thing above all else: trust."

The word hung in the air, heavy and unyielding. Some of the crew shifted uncomfortably in their seats, others kept their eyes locked on King, waiting for him to continue.

"Today," King continued, his tone hardening, "that trust was tested. We discovered a breach—an act of betrayal that could have cost us everything. The good news is, we stopped it. The bad news is, we're not finished. There's still a mission to complete, still threats out there waiting for us to falter."

He paused, letting his words sink in. "Now, I know what some of you are thinking. You're wondering if you can trust the man or woman sitting next to you. You're questioning everything. And I understand that. But let me make one thing clear: suspicion is the enemy of unity. And without unity, we are nothing. We are dead in the water."

The weight of his words pressed down on the room. King saw doubt in their eyes, but also resolve. These were skilled sailors, professionals, people who had been through fire and come out the other side. He just needed to remind them of who they were.

"We are the crew of the *Oregon*," King said, his voice rising. "We don't survive because we're lucky. We survive because we are disciplined, because we are a team. And no matter what challenges lie ahead, we will face them together. Trust isn't given; it's earned. And starting now, we earn it back."

A murmur of agreement rippled through the room. Some of the tension began to dissipate, though the wounds of doubt were far from healed. King knew this was only the first step, but it was a step forward nonetheless.

In the control room, Carter, Landry, and Green huddled over a new set of schematics. The modified communication systems had exposed a critical vulnerability, one they couldn't afford to leave unaddressed.

"We need a multilayered defense," Carter said, pointing to the network diagram. "If someone tries to infiltrate again, we'll know immediately."

Landry nodded, his fingers tapping against the edge of the table. "I can rewire the auxiliary circuits, create redundancies that flag unauthorized access."

"And we should lock down physical access points," Green added. "No one gets near the comm systems without clearance."

The three worked in unison, their focus unshaken. For all the tension and doubt that had plagued the *Oregon* earlier, this moment of collaboration felt like a turning point. They weren't just reacting to the sabotage; they were taking control.

Meanwhile, the crew began to feel the subtle shift in atmosphere. The unspoken accusations, the sidelong glances, and the undercurrent of suspicion were slowly being replaced by a renewed sense of purpose. Sailors worked side by side, their conversations less guarded, their movements more coordinated. They knew they couldn't afford to let doubt cripple them. If they were to succeed, they had to trust again.

In the torpedo bay, two junior crew members exchanged a quiet word of encouragement as they double-checked the equipment. In the galley, laughter broke out over a shared joke—tentative, but real. Even in the narrow corridors, where silence had reigned only hours before, there were signs of life returning to normal.

Later, Carter found herself in the control room with King. She handed him a report detailing the new security measures she, Landry, and Green had implemented.

"We've closed the gaps," she said. "If anyone tries something like this again, they won't get far."

King scanned the document, then looked up at her. "Good work. This isn't just about protecting our systems—it's about restoring confidence. And I think we're getting there."

Carter hesitated for a moment before speaking. "Do you think they'll hold together? The crew, I mean."

King's expression softened, though his resolve remained. "They will. They're stronger than they think. They just need to remember that."

As the *Oregon* sailed deeper into the unknown, the crew carried with them the scars of their ordeal—but also the lessons. Trust, fragile as it was, began to rebuild itself in the quiet moments of teamwork and shared purpose. The storm within had not passed entirely, but the first rays of sunlight were beginning to break through.

In the depths of the ocean, surrounded by darkness and danger, the *Oregon* found its strength not in the steel of its hull, but in the unity of its people. For they knew, now more than ever, that their survival depended on one another. Together, they would face whatever lay ahead. Together, they would prevail.

Part 8: The Hidden Menace

The glow of the dimmed lights in the control room cast long shadows across the walls, reflecting the gravity of the moment. The air was thick with tension, though the crew worked in silence, their movements precise, their focus absolute. Despite the brief sense of unity that Captain King had restored, a darker realization loomed—this battle was far from over.

Carter's eyes flitted across the glowing console, her fingers dancing over keys as she sifted through encrypted data. Her sharp gaze paused on a faint, irregular blip on the screen, a flicker so subtle it might have been dismissed as interference. But Carter knew better.

"Captain," she called, her voice cutting through the quiet. "I'm picking up a low-frequency signal. It's faint, but it's there."

King stepped closer, his presence steady, his mind racing as he studied the screen. "Could it be residual noise from the earlier transmissions?" he asked, though his instincts told him otherwise.

Carter shook her head, her tone resolute. "No, sir. This is deliberate. And it's moving—slowly, but it's there. It's not coming from us."

Across the room, Green, who had been monitoring navigation, leaned forward, his expression darkening. "If it's moving, then it's close. Too close."

King straightened, his voice calm but edged with steel. "Trace it. I want to know exactly where that signal is coming from."

Carter adjusted her equipment, isolating the frequency and triangulating its source. Each second felt like an eternity as the room held its collective breath, waiting for confirmation. The answer, when it came, was chilling.

"It's coming from the southeast," Carter said, her voice barely above a whisper. "Depth: 300 meters. It's another submarine."

The words hit like a thunderclap, reverberating through the room. The crew exchanged uneasy glances, but no one spoke. King's expression hardened, his mind calculating the implications. Another submarine meant more danger, more eyes watching, and perhaps more weapons aimed in their direction.

"Carter, can you identify it?" King asked, though he already suspected the answer.

She shook her head. "Not yet. The signal's too weak for a clear signature, but it's maintaining a steady course. If I had to guess…" She hesitated, the weight of her words evident. "It's one of theirs."

In the engineering bay, Landry stood hunched over a schematic of the *Oregon's* systems, his hands gripping the edges of the table. The discovery of another submarine had added a new layer of urgency to their work. He looked up as Green entered, his face a mask of grim determination.

"What's the word?" Landry asked.

Green crossed his arms, his voice low. "It's not confirmed yet, but Carter thinks it's Soviet. If they've got another boat out here, we're not just being hunted—we're being cornered."

Landry let out a low whistle, shaking his head. "Hell of a position we've landed ourselves in. And if they know where we are…"

"They don't yet," Green interrupted, his tone sharp. "But they will if we make the wrong move."

In the control room, King stood at the center, the weight of command pressing heavily on his shoulders. The faint hum of the submarine's systems filled the air, a backdrop to the thoughts racing through his mind. The enemy was closer than ever, and the *Oregon* was now navigating not just physical waters, but a sea of danger and deceit.

Carter's voice broke the silence. "Captain, I've cross-referenced the timing of the transmissions we intercepted. They align almost perfectly with the approach of this signal. Whoever was transmitting wasn't just feeding random data—they were guiding them. That submarine is here because of us."

King's jaw tightened. It wasn't just sabotage; it was precision. The enemy knew their moves, their position, perhaps even their intentions. The game had shifted, and the stakes were higher than ever.

He turned to the room, his voice steady but commanding. "Listen carefully. If we've got company, they're not here for a friendly chat. From this moment forward, assume every move we make is being watched. I want silent running protocols in full effect. No unnecessary transmissions, no deviations from course unless ordered."

The crew snapped to attention, their earlier doubts replaced by a renewed sense of purpose. They understood the gravity of the situation; hesitation was not an option.

As the *Oregon* maneuvered deeper into the shadowy depths, King remained at the helm, his gaze fixed on the map before him. The faint signal from the enemy submarine lingered in the corner of the screen, a constant reminder of the danger that lurked nearby.

"Captain," Carter said softly, approaching his side. "We've done all we can to secure the systems. But if they're this close, we need to prepare for the worst."

King nodded, his expression resolute. "We've been preparing since the day we set sail. Whatever's coming, we'll meet it head-on."

Part 1: The Trap Closes

The stillness of the deep was deceptive. Somewhere in the vast, dark expanse of the ocean, predators stalked their prey, and the *Oregon* lay caught in their crosshairs. The narrow passage of the undersea strait loomed ahead, its jagged walls a stark reminder of how precarious their position had become. A single misstep could spell disaster—not just from the Soviet submarine hunting them, but from the unforgiving terrain that surrounded them.

In the control room, tension hung like a thick fog. The faint, rhythmic pings of *Sokol's* active sonar echoed through the hydrophones, growing steadily louder. Each pulse sent ripples of unease through the crew, their eyes darting between monitors and instruments. The sound was an unspoken warning, a heartbeat of approaching danger.

"Active sonar," Carter's voice broke the silence, calm yet laced with urgency. Her gaze was fixed on her screen, the green glow reflecting the intensity in her eyes. "They're scanning aggressively. Range is closing—750 meters and counting."

Captain King stood at the center of the room, his broad shoulders squared, his expression unreadable. He didn't need Carter's report to feel the mounting threat; the very air seemed charged with it. He glanced at Green, who was hunched over the navigation console, his hands moving deftly as he calculated distances and angles.

"The terrain?" King asked, his voice steady despite the tension.

Green straightened, pointing to a holographic map of the seabed. The narrow strait was outlined, its walls rising sharply on either side. "It's tight. We've got about 20 meters clearance at this depth. One wrong move, and we're scraping rock—or worse."

King nodded, his jaw tightening. "And *Sokol*?"

"They're holding position for now, but that sonar sweep is moving closer," Carter replied. "If they get any stronger returns, they'll know we're here."

The submarine creaked softly as the hull adjusted to the pressure, the sound a low, haunting groan that seemed to echo the crew's unease. King turned his gaze to the periscope, though he knew there was nothing to see in the darkness outside. His thoughts raced. Moving now could risk detection, but remaining still might only delay the inevitable. It was a deadly gamble, and the stakes were rising with every passing moment.

"We hold," King said finally, his tone firm. "Minimize all noise. No unnecessary movements. Let's make them think they're chasing shadows."

The order was received with silent nods. Around him, the crew moved like clockwork, each action deliberate and precise. Yet the atmosphere was far from calm. In the confined space of the submarine, every sound— every tap on a console, every creak of the hull, every sharp intake of breath—seemed amplified, feeding the growing tension.

Carter's fingers danced over the controls as she monitored the sonar feed. The pulsing signals from *Sokol* painted a grim picture: the Soviet sub was probing the waters, its range tightening with each sweep. "They're adjusting their heading," she said quietly. "Range: 600 meters. Depth: matching ours."

King's eyes narrowed. The *Sokol* wasn't just hunting—they were zeroing in. He could almost feel the predatory intent of their captain, the calculated precision behind every move.

"Captain," Green said, his voice cutting through the tense silence. "If they move another 100 meters, they'll have us boxed in. We won't have room to maneuver."

King's mind worked quickly, weighing options that felt increasingly limited. He glanced at Carter. "Any sign of a thermal layer we can use?"

Carter shook her head. "Not at this depth. The water's too uniform. They'll see us clear as day if we move."

King's fist clenched at his side, though his voice remained calm. "Then we don't move. We wait."

The seconds stretched into minutes, each one heavier than the last. The *Oregon* lay silent, her engines idled to reduce noise. The faint glow of monitors illuminated the tense faces of the crew, their focus unwavering despite the weight of the moment.

And then it came: a sharper ping, louder than the others, echoing through the hydrophones with alarming clarity. Carter stiffened. "They've hit a stronger return. Range: 500 meters."

King's jaw tightened. He could feel the collective intake of breath around him, the crew bracing for what might come next. He straightened, his voice cutting through the tension like a blade. "Hold steady. No one breathes louder than they need to."

The *Oregon* remained motionless, a shadow in the depths. Outside, the cold, dark water carried the relentless pings of *Sokol's* sonar, each one a reminder that the hunter was closing in. And inside, the crew waited, the trap tightening around them with every passing second.

Part 2: The Snare Tightens

The oppressive silence in the *Oregon* was broken only by the relentless pings of *Sokol's* sonar. Each pulse rippled through the hull, reverberating like a slow, steady drumbeat—a predator marking the rhythm of its hunt. The narrow strait they occupied seemed to amplify the sound, bouncing the signals off jagged walls of rock and back toward them with unnerving clarity.

In the control room, the tension was palpable. Every creak of the submarine's structure felt amplified, every breath drawn seemed too loud. The pressure was mounting, not just from the surrounding ocean but from within the hearts of the crew.

Green leaned over the navigation console, his fingers tracing the contours of the undersea terrain displayed before him. His sharp eyes darted across the map, cataloging every ridge, crevice, and potential escape route. Finally, he spoke, his voice low but steady.

"There's a way out," he said, tapping a narrow gap at the far end of the map. "Here. But it's tight—barely wide enough for us to squeeze through. And the angle…" He trailed off, his expression grim.

Captain King stepped closer, his gaze fixed on the spot Green had indicated. "What's the margin for error?"

Green exhaled sharply. "Small. Very small. If we're off by even a few degrees, we'll scrape the hull—or worse, get wedged. And we're already making enough noise as it is."

The captain's eyes narrowed. The risk was immense, but so was the alternative: staying still and waiting for *Sokol* to zero in on them completely.

In the engineering bay, Landry wiped a bead of sweat from his brow as he monitored the status of the *Oregon's* power systems. The readings were grim. The submarine's batteries were nearly depleted, and the oxygen reserves were dwindling faster than anticipated. He muttered a quiet curse under his breath and activated the intercom.

"Captain," Landry's voice crackled through the control room speakers, carrying a tone of urgency. "We're running on fumes down here. Battery reserves are down to 15%, and oxygen levels aren't looking much better. If we don't move soon…"

"We're working on it," King replied curtly, cutting him off but not unkindly. He turned to Green, who was already recalculating the trajectory through the treacherous passage.

Landry's message hung in the air like a storm cloud. The crew exchanged uneasy glances, the gravity of their predicament sinking in deeper. Every second spent motionless felt like a countdown to disaster.

Carter's voice broke through the silence again, her tone sharp with tension. "Sokol's sonar sweep is intensifying. Range: 450 meters. They're focusing on this area. If they don't hear us, they'll find us just by proximity."

King clenched his fists, his mind racing. The decision weighed heavily: move and risk detection, or stay and risk entrapment. Both options seemed equally dire, and yet the clock was ticking relentlessly.

"Captain," Green said suddenly, his voice firm despite the pressure. "If we're going to make that passage, we need to move now. The current in the strait will only get stronger the longer we wait, and our power reserves won't hold out."

King met his eyes, the unspoken trust between them clear. Green's plan was a gamble—a dangerous one—but in this moment, it was the only shot they had.

The silence in the control room thickened as King made his decision. He turned to Carter. "Prepare to cut all non-essential systems. Landry, I need everything you've got left in the batteries for this maneuver."

Carter and Landry acknowledged the orders, their movements precise and deliberate despite the tension. The crew braced themselves, every muscle taut with anticipation.

As the *Oregon* began to inch forward, the water around it seemed to hum with the energy of the hunt. The sonar pings from *Sokol* were louder now, their rhythm faster, like a heartbeat accelerating with the thrill of the chase.

Inside, the crew moved as one, their focus razor-sharp. Yet the atmosphere was electric with tension. Every creak of the hull, every adjustment of the controls, every slight shift in the submarine's trajectory felt monumental.

"Steady," King murmured, his voice low but carrying authority. "We're not out yet."

But even as they moved, the weight of the ocean and the relentless pursuit of *Sokol* bore down on them. The trap was tightening, and the stakes had never been higher.

Part 3: The Evasion Plan

The control room buzzed with a low, focused intensity, like a hive of bees on the edge of action. Every officer was at their station, their eyes locked on screens and controls, their hands moving with precision. The *Oregon* had seconds, not minutes, to make a move before *Sokol's* sonar revealed their position. Captain King stood at the center, his presence commanding but calm, the weight of the moment visible only in the faint furrow of his brow.

"We're not outrunning them," King began, his voice steady as he addressed the crew. "Not like this. We'll use the terrain and let physics do the work. Engines to standby. We cut power, reduce noise, and ride the current out of this strait."

His words hung in the air for a moment. It was a plan that balanced brilliance and danger—surrendering control to the unpredictable currents of the ocean in a place where even the slightest miscalculation could be fatal.

Carter was the first to speak, her tone sharp with determination. "I'll need precise inputs for the navigation system," she said, her fingers already flying over the console. "I can map the flow of the current and calculate the trajectory, but the angle has to be perfect. If we're off by even half a degree…" She trailed off, the implications clear.

"We'll make it work," Green interjected, his voice calm but firm. He leaned over his station, rapidly inputting data and adjusting for the shifting currents. "The water's faster here—it'll give us the push we need, but the turbulence…" He glanced up at King. "It's going to get rough."

King nodded once, his decision already made. "Rough is better than dead. Do it."

In the engineering bay, Landry and his team worked with the controlled chaos of seasoned professionals. The hum of machinery mixed with the sharp clatter of tools as they prepared the *Oregon* for the shift to emergency power. Sweat dripped from Landry's forehead as he shouted instructions over the noise.

"Redirect all non-essential power to stabilizers and navigation. I want enough juice in the batteries to keep us from spinning out of control!"

One of the engineers, a wiry man with a streak of grease on his cheek, looked up from his console.
"Stabilizers are already strained from the last maneuver. We push them too hard, they'll blow."

"Then we make damn sure they don't blow," Landry shot back. "You've got five minutes—get it done."

Back in the control room, Carter's screen displayed a real-time projection of the *Oregon's* path. The jagged walls of the strait loomed on either side, and the highlighted currents twisted and turned like a serpent.

"This is the sweet spot," Carter said, pointing to a section of the map where the currents converged. "If we hit this angle, the flow will carry us through the narrowest section. But the turbulence here…" She traced a swirling line. "It's going to hit us like a freight train."

King's gaze was unflinching. "We don't have a choice. Gaps?"

"Two," Carter replied. "One here, the other 200 meters beyond. We miss the first, we're not making the second."

"Then we won't miss," King said simply, turning to Green. "You're guiding us through. Can you handle it?"

Green met his eyes, his usual smirk replaced with a look of unwavering focus. "Just don't flinch when I call the angles."

The crew moved as one, their movements synchronized by the shared understanding of what was at stake. The faint pings of *Sokol's* sonar grew louder, their rhythm quickening like a heartbeat sensing its prey.

"Engines ready for shutdown," Landry's voice came over the intercom. "We'll be on battery reserves for navigation and minimal systems only. Stabilizers are holding—for now."

"Good," King said, his gaze sweeping the room. "This is it, people. Execute."

Carter's hands danced across her console, inputting the final trajectory. Green's voice cut through the tense silence as he called out angles and adjustments, each command sharp and precise. Landry's team braced for the shift as the hum of the engines faded into silence, replaced by the low creak of the hull adjusting to the new pressures.

The *Oregon* began to drift, carried by the current. The initial motion was smooth, almost imperceptible, but then the turbulence hit. The submarine rocked violently, the force pressing the crew into their seats. Monitors flickered, and the low groan of the hull reverberated through the control room.

"Hold steady," King said, his voice cutting through the chaos. "Green?"

"Five degrees starboard," Green barked, his hands moving rapidly across the controls. "Bring us into the flow!"

Carter made the adjustment, her knuckles white against the edge of her console. "Trajectory holding. We're on course."

The *Oregon* shuddered again, the turbulence battering its frame as it was swept deeper into the strait. The sonar pings from *Sokol* began to fade, their clarity distorted by the chaotic currents.

"Current shift in ten seconds," Green called out. "Brace for impact!"

The submarine tilted sharply as the current dragged it into the next section of the strait. For a moment, the world seemed to hang in balance—every creak of the hull, every flicker of the instruments, every breath held by the crew a testament to the precariousness of their situation.

And then, with a final, jarring lurch, the turbulence eased. The *Oregon* stabilized, its path aligning with the projected trajectory. The sonar pings from *Sokol* were now faint and irregular, the terrain and currents working in the crew's favor.

"We're clear of the first gap," Carter reported, her voice steady despite the adrenaline coursing through her veins. "Second gap in 150 meters."

"Good work," King said, his tone calm but resolute. "Let's finish this."

The crew prepared for the next phase, their focus unbroken. The stakes were higher than ever, but for the first time in what felt like hours, the faint glimmer of hope began to shine through the tension. The *Oregon* wasn't safe yet—but they were still in the fight.

Part 4: The Breakthrough

The narrow strait yawned before the *Oregon*, its jagged walls looming like silent sentinels, waiting for the slightest misstep. The submarine's bulk seemed almost too large for the passage, its matte-black hull contrasting sharply with the sharp, unforgiving rock formations. Inside, the crew braced for what they all knew was coming. This was the moment where every calculation, every command, and every ounce of their courage would be put to the test.

"Approaching the passage," Carter reported, her voice a razor-thin thread of composure. "Depth clearance: minimal. Velocity: steady."

"Good," King replied, his gaze fixed on the projection of their course. "Green, keep us aligned. Landry, be ready to reroute power to stabilizers if we hit turbulence."

"Already on it," Landry's voice crackled over the intercom from engineering. "Don't expect miracles if we hit a rock, though. This baby wasn't built for bumper cars."

A faint ripple of nervous laughter passed through the control room, quickly replaced by focused silence.

As the *Oregon* entered the passage, the water around it churned with eddies and currents, creating an eerie dance of movement in the otherwise oppressive stillness. The submarine glided forward, her engines reduced to the barest whisper. The crew held their breath as the walls of the strait seemed to press closer, the distance between the hull and the rock narrowing with every meter.

"Five degrees starboard," Green commanded, his voice low and measured. His hands moved across the controls with surgical precision. "Hold steady… steady…"

The *Oregon* tilted slightly, responding to his touch. The shift was minute, almost imperceptible, but it made all the difference. The submarine slipped past an outcropping of sharp rock, the clearance so tight that Carter swore she could feel the vibration through the floor beneath her.

"Flow's picking up," Green muttered, his tone clipped. "We're riding it, but it's getting rougher. Stabilizers are going to feel this."

Suddenly, a sharp ping cut through the hydrophones—louder, more insistent than before. Carter's heart skipped a beat as she checked her readings.
"Sonar contact! *Sokol's* closing in fast. Range: 300 meters. They've locked onto our trajectory."

King's jaw tightened. "They're not letting us go without a fight."

And then came the sound they had all been dreading: the low, unmistakable thrum of a torpedo launch.

"Torpedo in the water!" Carter shouted. "Bearing: 180 degrees, speed: 50 knots. It's closing!"

The control room erupted into a flurry of activity. King barked orders, his voice cutting through the chaos like a whip.
"Green, evasive maneuvers! Landry, reinforce the stabilizers—keep us steady no matter what!"

The submarine veered sharply, the sudden movement sending a shudder through its frame. The torpedo's signature grew louder, its deadly approach a reminder of how little room for error they had.

"Impact in five seconds!" Carter's voice was taut with tension. "Four... three... two..."

The explosion rocked the *Oregon*, a deafening roar that reverberated through the hull. The shockwave hit like a sledgehammer, tossing the crew against their stations. Monitors flickered and dimmed, and the lights in the control room momentarily went out, plunging them into darkness.

"Damage report!" King demanded, gripping the edge of his station to steady himself.

"Stabilizers are offline!" Landry's voice came over the intercom, strained but clear. "We're compensating manually, but it's rough!"

Carter's hands flew over her console, recalibrating the sonar system. "Sonar's back up. The torpedo didn't hit directly—it detonated off the starboard side. Structural integrity holding, but we've got minor hull strain."

Green gritted his teeth as he fought to maintain control. "We're drifting into the wall. I need power to thrusters, now!"

"Diverting power!" Landry responded. The faint hum of the thrusters returned, pushing the *Oregon* back into alignment.

The submarine pressed forward, riding the turbulent flow of the strait. Behind them, the fading shockwaves of the explosion distorted the sonar pings from *Sokol*, buying the crew precious seconds to recover.

"We're clear of the worst turbulence," Carter reported, though her voice betrayed her exhaustion. "But *Sokol's* still tracking us."

King exhaled, his shoulders relaxing slightly. "They know we're here, but they'll have to guess where we're headed next. Let's keep it that way. Green, take us into the next current. Landry, monitor stabilizers—if they so much as blink, I want to know."

As the *Oregon* slid deeper into the passage, the crew regained their footing, their focus unbroken despite the harrowing ordeal. The faint trace of bubbles rose behind them, marking their path like a ghostly trail. Yet they were still alive, still moving forward.

In the shadows of the strait, the *Sokol* loomed, relentless in its pursuit. But for now, the *Oregon* had bought itself time—a fragile, fleeting victory in the deadly game they played.

Part 5: A Hair's Breadth from Death

The faint hum of the *Oregon's* battered systems filled the control room, underscoring the fragility of their situation. The submarine had slipped out of the immediate range of *Sokol's* sensors, the enemy's relentless sonar pings now distant murmurs swallowed by the surrounding ocean. But inside, the tension was far from abated. Every member of the crew felt the weight of their dwindling resources pressing down on them like the depths themselves.

Carter broke the uneasy silence.
"Captain," she began, her voice carefully controlled, though a tremor lingered beneath the surface. "Our oxygen reserves have dropped below critical. Estimated time remaining at current levels: forty minutes."

The words hit the room like a cold slap. Eyes darted toward King, awaiting his reaction. He remained still, his expression unreadable as he processed the grim reality.

Landry's voice crackled over the intercom from the engineering bay. "Battery levels are scraping the bottom too, Captain. We've got enough juice for minimal systems—navigation, sonar, maybe a short burst on the thrusters if we're lucky. But we're running on fumes here."

King nodded, absorbing the reports. The submarine was alive but barely holding on, and time was slipping through their fingers like grains of sand.

At the navigation console, Green adjusted his readings, his sharp eyes scanning the holographic map of the seabed. "Captain," he said, his tone urgent but measured, "I've been tracking the terrain ahead. There's a thermal layer about 200 meters below our current depth. It's not much, but it could mask our signature. *Sokol's* sonar would struggle to pick us up."

King moved to stand beside him, studying the map. The thermal layer was a potential shield, a natural barrier that might grant them precious moments of invisibility. But the descent to reach it would push the *Oregon* and her crew to their limits.

"What's the catch?" King asked, his voice calm, but his eyes sharp.

"The deeper we go, the more strain on the hull," Green admitted. "And the currents down there are unpredictable. If we lose control…" He didn't finish the sentence. He didn't need to.

Carter turned to face them, her expression serious. "Captain, staying here isn't an option. If our oxygen runs out, we're dead regardless. At least down there, we have a chance."

Landry's voice came through again. "Whatever we do, we need to do it fast. These systems won't hold up if we keep dragging this out."

King's gaze swept the room, taking in the faces of his crew. Tired, determined, but unwavering. They were holding the line, but he could see the strain creeping into their eyes. This decision wasn't just about survival; it was about giving them hope.

"All right," King said, his voice steady. "We take the dive. Green, plot the course and guide us down. Carter, keep monitoring *Sokol's* position—if they adjust, I want to know immediately. Landry, prep the systems for a controlled descent. We're going into the thermal layer."

There was no hesitation in their responses. The crew snapped into action, their movements precise despite the enormity of the task ahead.

The submarine began its slow descent, the hum of the thrusters barely audible over the creaking protest of the hull as it adjusted to the increasing pressure. The lights in the control room flickered momentarily, a grim reminder of how close they were to the edge.

"Depth: 400 meters," Carter reported, her voice steady but taut. "Thermal layer in 100 meters."

Green adjusted the course, his focus razor-sharp. "Currents are picking up. We're going to feel it soon."

And they did. The *Oregon* shuddered as it hit the first wave of turbulence, the water pushing against the hull like an unseen hand trying to tip them off balance.

"Stabilizers are holding," Landry reported, though his tone betrayed the effort it took to keep them that way. "Barely."

At 450 meters, the thermal layer began to register on the sensors—a faint, almost imperceptible shift in the water's composition.

"We're entering the layer," Carter announced. "Sonar returns are already starting to distort."

"Keep it steady," King instructed, his hands gripping the edge of his console. "We're not out of this yet."

The submarine slipped deeper, the murky water of the thermal layer enveloping it like a shroud. The noise of the outside world softened, muted by the natural barrier, and for the first time in what felt like hours, the relentless pings of *Sokol's* sonar began to fade.

"We're in," Green confirmed, exhaling a breath he hadn't realized he was holding. "Holding depth at 500 meters."

The room remained silent for a moment, the weight of what they had just accomplished settling over them. But the reprieve was fragile, and everyone knew it.

"Status on *Sokol*?" King asked.

Carter studied her console. "They've lost us—for now. They're adjusting their sweep, but the thermal layer's distortion is working in our favor."

King nodded, his face grim but resolute. "Good. Let's keep it that way. Maintain this depth and power down non-essentials. We need to conserve every bit of oxygen and energy we've got left."

The *Oregon* drifted in the silent embrace of the deep, hidden for the moment but still vulnerable. The crew exchanged weary but determined glances, their resolve unbroken. They had bought themselves a chance— a slim one, but a chance nonetheless. And as the submarine settled into the shadowy depths, Captain King allowed himself a brief moment of hope.

But he knew better than anyone: the hunt wasn't over yet.

Part 6: A Second Breath

The pressure inside the *Oregon* mirrored the crushing force of the ocean outside. Every creak of the hull, every flicker of the dimmed lights, and every sharp inhale of recycled air amplified the weight of their perilous situation. Yet, amidst the chaos of their descent, the crew moved with deliberate precision, their actions a symphony of unspoken coordination. Words were scarce—gestures, nods, and glances conveyed everything that needed to be said. In the silent depths, even a whisper felt like a roar.

The submarine glided deeper into the cold embrace of the thermal layer, its engines powered down to the barest whisper to conserve energy and avoid detection. Carter, her face illuminated by the pale green glow of her console, monitored the sonar. The signals from *Sokol* were erratic now, distorted by the natural barrier of the thermocline.

"Sonar returns are degrading further," she whispered, her voice barely audible in the tense stillness. "The thermal layer is scattering their pings. We might just lose them."

King stood behind her, his eyes fixed on the faint blips of the enemy's movements. "Let's make sure we give them nothing to find," he said, his tone a controlled calm that belied the razor edge of his focus.

In the engineering bay, Landry's team worked under dim emergency lights. Tools clinked softly, and the faint hum of machinery was the only background noise. Landry wiped his brow with the back of his hand, squinting at the readouts of the stabilizers. The shockwave from the torpedo had caused microfractures in the support systems, and the repairs were a delicate dance of precision and improvisation.

"Give me that sealant," he murmured to an assistant, pointing to a small canister. As the other man handed it over, Landry leaned closer to the damaged conduit. "If this doesn't hold, we're going to be in more trouble than we already are."

"Captain," his voice crackled over the intercom moments later, "we've patched the worst of it. Stabilizers are back at 70%. We can hold this depth, but I wouldn't recommend any sudden moves."

At the navigation station, Green was meticulously recalculating their position, his eyes darting between the map and the data feed. "We're at 500 meters," he announced softly. "The current's steady, and the turbulence is manageable. We're holding position."

Carter turned to him, her expression a mix of exhaustion and determination. "What about *Sokol*? Have they adjusted?"

"Not yet," Green replied, glancing at her monitor. "But they're not stupid. They'll change their sweep pattern soon enough."

The submarine finally stabilized, its hull groaning softly as it settled into the thermal layer. For the first time in hours, the frantic energy of the control room gave way to a tentative calm. Carter exhaled slowly, her shoulders relaxing slightly as she continued to monitor the sonar. The blips from *Sokol* were faint now, their signals disoriented by the water's shifting temperature and density.

"They're turning," Carter reported. "Changing course. Looks like they're moving north."

A collective breath seemed to ripple through the room. The relentless hunter had lost their scent—for now.

King straightened, his gaze sweeping the room. "Good work, everyone," he said, his voice carrying a rare note of praise. "But we're not out of the woods yet. Landry, keep monitoring the systems. Carter, stay on sonar. Green, start charting a new course. We need to get clear of this area before they decide to double back."

The crew nodded in silent acknowledgment, their movements gaining a steadiness that came from the flicker of hope now burning within them.

For a brief moment, the control room settled into a quiet rhythm. The dim lights cast long shadows, and the soft hum of the systems provided a fragile sense of normalcy. Yet, beneath the surface, every member of the crew remained acutely aware of the precariousness of their survival.

In his mind, King knew they had only bought time. The *Oregon* was still vulnerable, its resources dangerously low, and the shadow of *Sokol* lingered like a phantom in the depths. But for now, the immediate threat had receded, and his crew had proven their mettle once again.

As the submarine drifted silently in the cold, shadowed embrace of the thermal layer, King allowed himself a single thought: they had earned this moment. A brief reprieve, a second breath in an unforgiving ocean.

But the chase wasn't over, and he knew the next move would be just as critical as the last.

For now, they would hold their position, invisible in the depths. But the *Oregon* was far from safe, and the hunt was far from finished.

Part 7: The Aftermath

The *Oregon* lay suspended in the cold embrace of the thermal layer, a silent shadow in an ocean of secrets. Inside, the tension that had gripped the crew during the harrowing descent began to dissipate, replaced by an almost eerie calm. The control room was quieter now, the urgent commands and hurried movements replaced with the soft hum of systems running on emergency power and the occasional creak of the hull as it adjusted to the immense pressure.

King stood at the center, his gaze sweeping the room. He could see the exhaustion etched into the faces of his crew—the sheen of sweat on foreheads, the tight set of jaws, the trembling hands that betrayed adrenaline crashes. And yet, they were steady, every person at their station, still ready to respond if the need arose.

"Status," King said finally, his voice breaking the silence but carrying none of the sharp edge it usually held.

Carter, seated at her console, glanced up. Her face was pale, but her expression was calm and focused.
"Sonar confirms *Sokol* has shifted course. They're moving north, well out of detection range. For now, we're safe."

A flicker of relief passed through the room, but it was fleeting. Carter continued, her tone sobering.
"But we're not in the clear, Captain. The data from earlier transmissions suggests the Soviets have dispatched reinforcements. A fleet, possibly including other subs. If they triangulate our position…" She let the thought hang in the air.

King nodded, his expression grim but resolute. "Then we'll make sure they don't. Good work, Carter. Keep monitoring their movements. Let me know if anything changes."

"Landry, damage assessment?" King turned his attention to the engineering officer, whose voice came through the intercom from the lower decks.

"Well, Captain," Landry began, a faint edge of weariness in his tone, "it's a miracle we're still in one piece after that torpedo. Stabilizers are back up, but they're fragile. The microfractures in the hull aren't critical—yet. Batteries are down to 12%, and at this depth, the strain is eating into what little juice we have left. Oxygen reserves are holding steady for now, but we're living on borrowed time. If we don't surface or find another solution soon, we're going to run out of options."

"Can we push deeper if we have to?" King asked.

Landry's pause was telling. "We *can*, but I wouldn't bet on surviving it. This girl wasn't built to hang out at these depths for long, let alone go deeper. If it comes to that, I'd start saying your prayers."

A faint chuckle rippled through the crew, not from humor but from the shared weight of their situation. King allowed himself a small, almost imperceptible smile. "Noted. Keep me updated on those stabilizers. Good work, Landry."

King stepped away from the center of the room and motioned for Green and Carter to join him in a huddle near the navigation console. Despite the fatigue written across their faces, they moved with the precision of professionals.

"We need a plan," King said quietly, his tone firm but measured. "Carter, what's our window before the reinforcements can lock onto us?"

"Best guess, 12 hours," she replied. "But that's assuming they're moving at a standard speed. If they're pushing, it could be less."

Green leaned over the map display, tracing a path with his finger. "We could use the thermocline to buy us time. Follow its contours and slip out of their likely search patterns. It'll be slow, but it'll keep us hidden."

King considered this, nodding. "Do it. Plot the course. I want us ready to move in fifteen minutes."

Before stepping back to the center of the room, King addressed them both. "You've both done excellent work today. I know the stakes are high, but we're still here because of the decisions you made. Thank you."

Neither replied, but their faint nods and the glimmer of pride in their eyes spoke volumes.

Once the immediate tasks were underway, King pressed the intercom, his voice carrying through every corner of the sub. "Attention, crew of the *Oregon*. I know the last few hours have been some of the toughest we've faced. You've been tested in ways most sailors never will, and you've proven yourselves time and time again. Because of you, we're still alive. You've shown courage, skill, and determination under pressure, and for that, I thank you."

A pause hung in the air, and when King continued, his tone grew more resolute.
"But this isn't over. The Soviets are still out there, and the challenges ahead will be even greater than those behind us. I trust every one of you to rise to the occasion. Together, we'll navigate through this and come out stronger. Stay sharp. King out."

In the quiet that followed, a sense of renewed focus settled over the submarine. The crew straightened at their stations, their exhaustion momentarily eclipsed by a collective determination.

King returned to his post, his mind already working through the next steps. The *Oregon* was battered, its resources stretched thin, but they weren't beaten. Not yet. In the depths of the ocean, with the shadows of the enemy looming, the battle was far from over—but for now, they had time to prepare.

And sometimes, in the unforgiving theater of war, time was the greatest victory of all.

Chapter 7: Revelation

Part 1: A New Puzzle

The soft glow of the monitors in the communications room barely cut through the dimness of the *Oregon's* interior. Lieutenant Carter sat at her station, her sharp eyes scanning rows of data. Her fingers danced across the keyboard, isolating fragments of transmissions left behind by the recently exposed spy. The lines of code and waveforms felt like a trail of breadcrumbs, scattered and faint but leading somewhere.

She leaned closer to the screen, her brow furrowed. The first spy's transmissions had been erratic yet calculated, slipping just under the radar. But now, something else was surfacing—a secondary pattern, faint but distinct, emerging from the chaos. The intervals between transmissions were too precise to be coincidence, too deliberate to be dismissed as interference.

Her heart began to race as the pieces started fitting together. *This wasn't just one person's work. Someone else is pulling the strings—or still transmitting.*

"Unbelievable," she muttered under her breath, her voice barely audible above the steady hum of the submarine's systems. She highlighted a section of the data and cross-referenced it with the crew's activity logs. Her stomach dropped as a chilling realization took hold: the timing of these transmissions aligned suspiciously with the movements of another crew member.

Carter's instincts screamed at her to act, but she knew better than to jump to conclusions. Accusations without evidence could unravel what little cohesion the crew had left after the last ordeal. *No room for error, no room for panic,* she reminded herself.

Minutes later, she stood outside the captain's quarters, her pulse steady despite the weight of what she was about to reveal. The faint creak of the metal frame as she knocked seemed deafening in the silence.

"Enter," came King's voice, calm but edged with authority.

She stepped inside, the door hissing shut behind her. The captain sat at his desk, charts and navigation data spread before him like a battlefield map. He glanced up, his sharp gaze meeting hers.

"Lieutenant Carter," he said, gesturing for her to sit. "You look like you've seen a ghost."

Carter didn't smile at his attempt to lighten the tension. "Captain, we might still have a problem."

That got his attention. He leaned forward, resting his forearms on the desk. "Go on."

Carter placed a tablet on the desk and pulled up the data she'd been analyzing. "This is a comparison of the transmissions we intercepted from the first spy and new activity I discovered in the last twelve hours." She pointed to a series of waveforms. "At first glance, it's easy to miss, but these intervals—these timings—are too precise to be random noise. They're deliberate."

King studied the screen, his expression unreadable. "What's your assessment?"

"These transmissions coincide with specific movements and actions of another crew member," she continued, her voice steady despite the implications of her words. "Whoever it is, they're careful. This isn't sloppiness. It's calculated."

King's jaw tightened, his mind already working through the potential fallout. "Do you have a name?"

"Not yet," Carter admitted. "I need more time to isolate the exact source. But I'm confident there's a second agent onboard."

King leaned back in his chair, his eyes narrowing as he processed the information. The betrayal of the first spy had been a heavy blow to morale, but the thought of a second one—someone who had been quietly continuing the work—was an even greater threat.

"We can't afford to let this get out," he said finally. "If the crew gets wind of this, it'll tear us apart. Keep this between us for now. What's your plan?"

Carter straightened. "I'll continue monitoring the transmissions and cross-referencing with crew activity logs. If we can narrow it down, I'll need Green's help to establish visual confirmation or trace physical movements. We'll need to act fast once we identify them."

"Agreed," King said, nodding. "Coordinate with Green discreetly. And Carter…" He paused, meeting her gaze. "Good work. But be careful. Whoever this is, they're dangerous, and they know we're closing in."

As Carter left the room, the weight of the captain's words settled on her. The walls of the *Oregon* seemed to close in around her as she made her way back to the communications station. The air felt heavier, the shadows deeper. Somewhere on this submarine, hidden among the faces she saw every day, was someone working against them.

Her resolve hardened. This wasn't just a matter of duty anymore—it was personal. She would find them, and she would stop them before they could put the entire mission, and every life onboard, in jeopardy.

The silent hunt had begun.

Part 2: The Silent Enemy

The air inside the *Oregon* was heavy with unspoken tension. Lieutenant Carter sat at her station, her eyes darting between the screen and the activity log in her hand. The pattern was emerging, slowly but surely—a shadow moving behind the routines of the crew. Her suspicions had settled on one individual, but there were no hard facts to confirm it. Just a series of unsettling coincidences and a creeping certainty in her gut.

Across the control room, the suspect sat at his post, seemingly calm, his movements precise yet unremarkable. Too unremarkable. Carter's gaze lingered on him, her mind racing. *He's too careful. Every action is measured, deliberate—like he's hiding in plain sight.*

The shift had been uneventful so far, but murmurs were beginning to ripple through the crew. A set of storage lockers in one of the engineering bays had been left unsecured—something that never happened under normal conditions. A few consoles had glitched briefly, their data streams momentarily disrupted. Minor issues on the surface, but together, they painted a picture of subtle sabotage.

Carter's lips pressed into a thin line. *He's testing the waters, seeing what he can get away with without drawing too much attention.*

She moved across the room to where Lieutenant Green was bent over a map display. His brow furrowed as he adjusted the plotting tools, but he glanced up when Carter approached.

"Green," she said in a low voice, her tone tight with purpose, "I need your help."

He straightened, his sharp features betraying curiosity and concern. "What's going on?"

Carter glanced around to make sure no one was paying attention. "I've been tracking the transmissions. I think I've narrowed it down to one of the crew."

Green's expression darkened. "You're sure?"

"Not yet," Carter admitted. "But the signs are there. It's not just the transmissions—there's been odd behavior, minor disruptions. Nothing we can pin on anyone directly, but enough to know someone's working behind the scenes."

Green folded his arms, his gaze shifting briefly toward the suspect before returning to Carter. "If you're right, then we can't risk confronting them outright. Not without proof."

"Exactly," Carter said. "That's where you come in. We need to keep a close eye on him. I want to set up covert surveillance—monitor his movements, track what he accesses."

Green nodded slowly, his mind already working through the plan. "We need to be careful. If he catches on, he might try to destroy evidence or sabotage critical systems."

Carter's jaw tightened, her resolve hardening.
"I know. That's why we need to act now, before he makes his next move. If we wait too long, he could pass information or cause even more damage."

The two officers quickly devised a plan. Green would reroute a portion of the internal security feeds to a secure console, allowing them to monitor the suspect's activity without alerting the rest of the crew. Meanwhile, Carter would continue analyzing the transmissions, looking for any additional patterns or evidence to solidify their case.

Later that evening, as the ship settled into the quiet rhythm of its night cycle, Carter and Green executed their plan. The suspect moved through the submarine with a precision that bordered on mechanical, his actions neither hurried nor hesitant. He interacted with his colleagues casually, exchanged nods and words with just the right amount of engagement to avoid suspicion.

But to Carter, every gesture felt like a mask. She watched as he entered the engineering bay, lingering just a second too long near the coolant system before moving on. The data feed showed a slight fluctuation in the system moments after he left—barely enough to register, but Carter noticed.

Green's voice crackled softly over her headset. "He's good, I'll give him that. But no one's perfect."

Carter allowed herself a grim smile. "We'll see about that."

The silent hunt continued through the night. The crew, unaware of the invisible net tightening around the suspect, carried on with their duties, their whispers of unease subdued but persistent. Carter knew they couldn't keep this up forever. Eventually, he would either make a mistake—or force their hand.

For now, all she could do was watch, wait, and stay one step ahead of the silent enemy lurking among them.

Part 3: Panic and Sabotage

The steady rhythm of the *Oregon's* machinery was abruptly interrupted by a sharp alarm that echoed through the corridors. The control room burst into motion as warning lights flickered to life, casting the space in an eerie red glow. Lieutenant Landry's voice crackled over the intercom, tense but composed.

"Captain, we've got a coolant flow irregularity in the secondary system. It's showing a drop in pressure."

Captain King shot a glance at Carter, who was already leaning over her console, checking for additional anomalies. Her fingers moved rapidly across the controls, but her mind was elsewhere, replaying the suspect's recent movements.

"Landry," King said, his tone clipped, "how bad is it?"

"Localized for now, sir," Landry replied, the strain in his voice evident. "But if the flow continues to drop, we're looking at a chain reaction. The reactor will overheat."

King stood, his presence commanding attention as the crew awaited his orders. "Landry, isolate the affected area and reroute the flow to the primary system. Carter, monitor for any signs of cascading failures. We can't afford for this to spread."

"Yes, sir," they replied in unison.

As the crew sprang into action, Carter's mind raced. The timing of the malfunction was too convenient, too deliberate. The coolant system had been inspected earlier that day—she had seen the report herself. It was flawless then.

Her eyes flicked to the surveillance feed, searching for anything unusual. There, in the corner of the screen, she spotted him. The suspect, moving swiftly and with purpose, disappeared down a corridor leading to the maintenance hatch just moments before the alarm sounded.

"Captain," she said, her voice sharp with urgency, "we may have a bigger problem."

King turned to her, his expression darkening. "What is it, Carter?"

"The timing of this malfunction," she said, pointing to the surveillance feed, "isn't a coincidence. That corridor leads to the coolant control manifold. He was there right before the system flagged the irregularity."

King's jaw tightened, his mind processing the implications. "You're saying he sabotaged it?"

"I can't prove it," Carter admitted, her tone bitter with frustration. "But it's too precise to be anything else."

Landry's voice interrupted the conversation. "Captain, rerouting's taking longer than expected. Something's jammed the valves—we're trying to clear it manually."

King swore under his breath. "Carter, keep tracking him. Landry, prioritize clearing that system. If the reactor goes, we're done."

"Yes, sir," Landry replied, his tone grim.

The tension in the room was palpable as Carter continued monitoring both the coolant system and the suspect's movements. He had vanished from the immediate camera feeds, slipping into the blind spots of the *Oregon's* surveillance network. Her frustration mounted.

"Where are you?" she muttered under her breath, her eyes scanning every inch of the screen.

Meanwhile, in the engineering bay, Landry and his team worked frantically to clear the jammed valves. Sweat dripped down their faces as they struggled with the stubborn mechanisms, the heat from the reactor adding to the already stifling atmosphere.

"Come on, come on," Landry muttered, his hands slick with grease as he wrenched at a valve with all his strength.

Back in the control room, Carter's console lit up with a new alert. "Captain, we've got another pressure drop in the primary system. It's spreading."

King's fist clenched as he processed the escalating crisis. "Landry, status?"

"We're close, sir," came the strained reply. "Just need a few more minutes."

"We don't have a few minutes," King barked.

Carter's gaze snapped to a new camera feed, catching a fleeting glimpse of the suspect entering a restricted maintenance hatch. Her breath hitched. "There! He's heading into the auxiliary control room."

King's expression hardened. "Get Green and secure that room. Now."

As Carter relayed the order, the weight of the situation pressed heavily on her. The sabotage was no longer just a theory—it was happening, and if they didn't act fast, it would spiral into catastrophe.

The hum of the *Oregon's* systems seemed louder than ever, a reminder of the delicate balance that kept them alive. Carter knew one thing for certain: the silent enemy among them was no longer hiding. He had made his move, and now it was their turn to strike back.

Part 4: The Invisible Threat

The dim red glow of emergency lights painted the cramped corridors of the *Oregon*, their flickering illumination casting elongated, distorted shadows. The air felt heavier now, both from the palpable tension and the dwindling oxygen reserves. The crew moved like ghosts, their whispers and muted movements a stark contrast to the chaos unraveling beneath the surface.

Carter's console displayed a chaotic cascade of data. She squinted at the screen, her fingers flying across the keyboard as she parsed through corrupted files and fragmented logs. Among the wreckage, a faint digital footprint emerged—a trace of deliberate tampering.

"There," she murmured, her voice barely audible over the hum of the systems. The suspect had tried to erase his tracks, but haste had left pieces of the puzzle behind. Incomplete fragments of commands and access points painted a picture of someone navigating the ship's network with precision. It wasn't a random act of desperation; it was methodical, calculated.

"Captain," Carter called, her voice sharp and steady. "He's tampered with the logs, but I've found residual traces. He accessed the coolant systems directly, then tried to wipe the logs from auxiliary control. He didn't finish the job."

King loomed over her console, his presence a steadying force amid the storm. "Can you track him?"

Carter hesitated for only a moment. "Not directly, but I can predict his route. He's heading for one of the maintenance hatches—probably trying to reach the strategic systems near the aft section."

"Then we'll cut him off," King said, turning toward Green, who was already hovering near the navigation station. "Green, map the quickest route to intercept him. We can't let him reach the propulsion or reactor controls."

Green nodded, his fingers deftly manipulating the controls. The submarine's schematics unfolded across the screen, a maze of tight corridors and access points. His brow furrowed as he traced the suspect's likely path.

"He'll have to take this junction," Green said, pointing to a critical intersection near the reactor's primary cooling intake. "If we seal the bulkhead here, we can force him toward an isolated section."

The captain's voice cut through the growing tension. "Do it. Carter, stay on the logs. If he left any more breadcrumbs, I want to know where they lead."

The crew around them moved with focused urgency, but the tight quarters and mounting tension were beginning to wear on them. Every breath seemed heavier, every sound amplified. Landry's team in the engineering bay was still battling the sabotage's effects, and the limited oxygen reserves were becoming an unspoken weight pressing on everyone's shoulders.

As Green coordinated with the security team to seal the bulkheads, Carter zeroed in on the suspect's remaining traces. Her heart pounded as she uncovered a series of access commands aimed at the propulsion systems.

"He's trying to destabilize the ship's thrusters," she said, her voice clipped. "If he manages to disable propulsion, we'll lose our ability to maneuver—and he'll have free reign to cause more damage."

"Not on my watch," Green muttered. He moved quickly, checking the feeds from the remaining operational cameras. He caught a flash of movement—just a shadow, disappearing into the corridor near the sealed bulkhead.

"He's there," Green said, pointing to the screen. "We've got him cornered, but he knows this ship as well as we do. He'll try to find another way out."

King's voice remained calm but commanding. "No one knows this ship better than us. We'll use that to our advantage."

The corridors of the *Oregon* felt even tighter now, the walls seeming to close in as the hunt continued. The invisible threat that had haunted them for days was now tangible, its shadow slipping through the ship like a predator in the dark.

Carter clenched her jaw, her focus unshakable. The suspect had made his move, but he had underestimated their resolve. They were closing in, and the noose was tightening. There was no room for error—not now, not ever.

Green's voice came over the intercom, steady and sure. "We've got him. Bulkheads are sealed, and he's boxed in near the auxiliary control junction. There's nowhere left for him to go."

Carter allowed herself a small breath of relief, but the battle was far from over. The suspect might have been cornered, but he was still dangerous— and desperate people rarely surrendered without a fight.

The trap was set. Now, they just had to spring it.

Part 5: Confrontation

The tension in the auxiliary control room was palpable, the air thick with the hum of the submarine's systems and the low thrum of distant machinery. Carter and Green moved quietly, their footsteps barely audible against the metal grating beneath their feet. The emergency lights flickered, casting intermittent shadows that seemed to shift and move like specters in the confined space.

Ahead of them, the suspect crouched over a console, his fingers working furiously on the keyboard. The dim light illuminated his face, beads of sweat glistening on his brow as he typed command after command. A faint green light blinked on the terminal—a sign that he was attempting to establish a connection.

Carter's pulse quickened as she observed the scene from the corner of the room. She motioned to Green, her hand a silent command. He nodded, moving to flank the suspect while Carter approached from the other side, her heart pounding in her chest. The suspect hadn't noticed them yet, too engrossed in his desperate task.

"Step away from the console!" Carter's voice cut through the room, sharp and commanding.

The suspect froze, his hands hovering over the keys. Slowly, he turned, his face a mask of defiance and fear.

"You don't understand," he said, his voice low and taut. "It's not what you think."

Green stepped closer, his presence looming. "We understand enough. Stand down and move away—now."

For a moment, the suspect hesitated, his eyes darting between the two officers. Then, with a sudden burst of movement, he lunged toward the console, his hand slamming down on a sequence of keys.

"Stop him!" Carter shouted, rushing forward. Green reacted instantly, grabbing the suspect by the arm and yanking him away from the terminal. The man struggled, his strength fueled by desperation.

"You don't know what you're doing!" the suspect snarled, his voice rising as he twisted against Green's grip.

Carter moved to the console, her fingers flying across the keyboard as she attempted to undo the commands the suspect had entered. A warning flashed on the screen: **"Data transfer in progress."**

"Green, keep him away!" Carter barked, her focus laser-sharp. She typed furiously, bypassing the encryption the suspect had initiated. The transfer was incomplete, but she could feel the seconds slipping away like grains of sand in an hourglass.

Behind her, the struggle intensified. The suspect broke free from Green's grasp and lunged toward the console again, his hands outstretched. Carter barely had time to react. She turned, her arm coming up to block him, her determination overriding her fear.

"You're not winning this," she said through gritted teeth, holding her ground as the man pushed against her.

The door to the room hissed open, and Captain King stepped inside, his presence filling the space like a storm rolling in.

"What the hell is going on here?" King's voice was ice-cold, slicing through the chaos.

The suspect froze, his eyes wide as he realized the game was over. Green took the opportunity to grab him again, this time forcing him to the ground.

"He was initiating a data transfer," Carter said, still breathless but resolute. She gestured to the console. "I stopped it, but he nearly succeeded."

King stepped forward, his eyes locking onto the suspect, who glared back defiantly.

"You've endangered this entire mission," King said, his voice low and dangerous. "Give me one reason not to treat this as treason of the highest order."

The suspect didn't respond, his jaw set and his gaze unwavering.

"Secure him," King ordered, stepping back. "And make sure he can't access anything else. Carter, what's the status of the data?"

"It's incomplete," Carter replied, her hands still working to ensure the transfer was fully terminated. "But I'll need time to make sure nothing was sent out."

King nodded, his expression grim. "Do it. Green, take him to the brig. I'll deal with him later."

As the suspect was hauled out of the room, Carter turned back to the console, her fingers trembling slightly as the adrenaline began to wear off. She knew the danger wasn't entirely over—there was still the possibility that fragments of data had slipped through.

King placed a steadying hand on her shoulder. "Good work, Carter. You stopped him when it mattered."

She nodded, swallowing hard. "Thank you, sir. But this isn't over. Not yet."

"No," King agreed, his voice heavy. "But we'll be ready for whatever comes next."

The room fell silent again, save for the faint hum of the systems. The immediate threat had been neutralized, but the weight of what had just happened hung over them like a storm cloud, a reminder that their fight was far from over.

Part 6: The Chain of Exposures

The dimly lit interrogation room felt oppressively small, the hum of the submarine's systems seeping through the walls like an ominous reminder of their precarious position. Captain King stood tall, his silhouette cutting a formidable figure against the faint glow of the room's single console. Across the table sat the second spy, his expression blank, but his clenched fists betrayed his internal turmoil.

King leaned forward, his eyes sharp and unyielding. "We already know about the coolant sabotage and the failed transmission. What we don't know is who else you've been communicating with."

The spy didn't flinch, his lips pressed into a stubborn line. Silence filled the room like a tangible force.

In the adjacent control room, Carter worked feverishly at her station, her fingers flying across the keyboard as she pieced together the remnants of the deleted logs. Each recovered fragment painted a clearer picture of the second spy's activities. She muttered to herself, her focus absolute.

"There," she said, her voice cutting through the quiet. "I've got something."

Landry, who had been monitoring the coolant system diagnostics nearby, stepped closer. "What is it?"

Carter pointed to the screen, highlighting a recovered string of data. "These are transmission logs. He was attempting to send detailed navigational data—our position, projected course, and even system vulnerabilities. If this had gone through..." She trailed off, the implications hanging heavy in the air.

Landry's face darkened. "They'd have known exactly where to strike. We wouldn't have stood a chance."

Back in the interrogation room, King's patience was wearing thin. He crossed his arms, his voice low and cutting. "You're in a sinking ship, sailor. Whatever you thought you were achieving, it's over. The question now is whether you go down with it or give me something useful."

The spy finally shifted, his jaw tightening. "You don't understand. It wasn't supposed to go this far. They weren't supposed to know..."

King's eyes narrowed. "Who? Who weren't they supposed to know about?"

The spy hesitated, his resolve cracking under the weight of King's gaze. "I wasn't working with the first guy," he said, his voice low and hoarse. "We didn't even know about each other. Different lines, different handlers. They didn't want us connected."

In the control room, Carter continued to dig deeper into the logs. She pulled up a secondary file, its encrypted structure more advanced than the first. Her hands moved faster, breaking through layers of security protocols until the file opened.

Her breath hitched. "Captain," she said through the comms, her voice taut with urgency.

King pressed his earpiece. "Go ahead."

"I've recovered more data. This wasn't just about coolant sabotage or a simple course leak. He was transmitting long-term patterns—our patrol areas, sonar activity logs. This information isn't just tactical—it's strategic. They could use this to predict every move we make."

King's jaw tightened. "Understood. Keep digging."

Landry interjected, his voice grim. "Captain, about the sabotage. The system wasn't just damaged—it was primed for failure. If we hadn't caught it when we did, the cooling systems would have collapsed entirely. It wouldn't have just been a setback; it would've been catastrophic."

The room fell silent for a moment as the gravity of the revelation sank in.

King turned back to the spy, his voice a low growl. "You were prepared to kill every man on this ship to complete your mission. Tell me why."

The spy's mask of defiance cracked, his eyes flicking between King and the console. "It wasn't supposed to be like this. The data was meant to be collected, nothing more. The sabotage... that wasn't part of my orders. It was improvised."

King's gaze hardened. "Improvised or not, you've endangered this entire crew. And now you're going to tell me everything, or I'll make sure you never leave this room."

Meanwhile, Carter pieced together the final fragments of the deleted logs, her heart sinking as the full scope of the betrayal came into focus. "Captain," she said, her voice tight. "The data he was transmitting—it includes more than just our ship. There's information on allied movements, rendezvous points… they were preparing for something bigger."

King straightened, his mind racing. The implications were staggering. This wasn't just an isolated act of sabotage. It was part of a coordinated effort, one that extended far beyond the *Oregon*.

"Good work, Carter," he said, his voice steady despite the storm brewing in his mind. "Keep that data secure. We'll need to transmit it back to command as soon as possible."

Turning back to the spy, King leaned in close, his voice cold as steel. "You've done enough damage. But I promise you this—whatever you were planning, it ends here."

The spy looked away, his silence speaking volumes. The pieces of the puzzle were finally falling into place, but King knew this was just the beginning. The enemy was still out there, watching, waiting. And now, they had to prepare for what was coming next.

The room fell silent again, the hum of the submarine's systems a stark reminder of the delicate balance they had to maintain. The stakes had never been higher, but the crew of the *Oregon* was ready to face whatever lay ahead. They had to be.

Part 7: Lessons in Teamwork

The hum of the *Oregon's* systems was a comforting backdrop as the crew worked to steady the ship after the chaos of the past few hours. In the command center, screens glowed softly, casting a serene, almost unreal calm over the room—a stark contrast to the storm they had just weathered.

Carter stood over her console, a furrow of concentration on her brow as she adjusted parameters for the submarine's communication systems. Beside her, Green leaned on the edge of the desk, his sharp eyes scanning the schematics she had pulled up. The two worked in tandem, their synergy apparent in the way they passed ideas back and forth without the need for elaborate explanations.

"We need a secondary encryption layer," Carter said, not looking up. "Something decentralized, so even if someone breaches one system, they can't access the rest."

Green nodded, reaching for a stylus and making notes on a nearby tablet. "We could partition the channels. Route critical transmissions through a ghost network—completely invisible unless you know exactly where to look."

"That'll take time to set up," Carter said, her fingers still moving. "But it's worth it."

"We don't have much of a choice," Green replied, his tone grim. "The alternative is letting this happen again."

Across the ship, Landry was knee-deep in the engineering bay, his hands covered in grease as he directed his team. The faint smell of overheated metal and machinery filled the air, but the engineers moved with precision, each task part of a larger effort to secure the ship's critical systems.

Landry stood back for a moment, surveying their work with a practiced eye. "Alright, listen up," he said, his voice carrying authority without harshness. "We're implementing new inspection protocols, starting now. Every critical system gets a full diagnostic twice per shift. No shortcuts. No exceptions."

One of the junior engineers looked up, sweat streaking his face. "Twice per shift, sir? With our current workload, that's—"

"I know it's a lot," Landry interrupted, his tone softening. "But this isn't negotiable. We were lucky this time. Next time, we might not be. Got it?"

The engineer nodded, his expression serious. "Understood, sir."

In the briefing room, Captain King stood before his senior officers. The room was quiet, save for the soft rustling of uniforms as the crew adjusted in their seats. The events of the day hung heavy in the air, but there was also a sense of relief—a fragile calm born from their survival.

King's voice was steady but carried a weight that drew everyone's attention. "What we've just been through wasn't just a test of our systems or our protocols. It was a test of us—our ability to function as a unit under pressure."

He paused, letting the words sink in before continuing. "We've taken hits, and we've seen the cracks in our armor. But we've also seen what this crew is capable of. Every one of you stepped up today, and because of that, we're still here."

Carter exchanged a glance with Green, a faint smile passing between them.

King's gaze swept the room. "We're not done yet. There's still work to do—repairs to make, protocols to implement, and trust to rebuild. But I've seen what this crew is made of, and I know we'll come out of this stronger."

After the briefing, Carter and Green returned to their stations, the faint hum of the ship a reminder of the ever-present stakes.

"Think we'll ever get a quiet day?" Green asked, his tone light but with an edge of fatigue.

Carter smirked, her fingers still flying across the keyboard. "On this ship? Not a chance."

In the engineering bay, Landry finished his rounds, his team dispersing to their tasks. He placed a hand on the nearest bulkhead, feeling the faint vibrations beneath his palm. It was as if the *Oregon* itself was alive, holding its breath along with the crew.

"All right, girl," he muttered to the submarine. "Let's keep it together a little longer."

Back in the command center, King stood alone for a moment, his hands resting on the console. The weight of command was always heavy, but today it felt just a little lighter. The crew had proven their mettle, and while the road ahead was still uncertain, he knew they would face it together.

The soft glow of the monitors reflected in his eyes as he straightened his shoulders. The *Oregon* had survived the storm, and as long as this crew was on board, it would weather whatever came next.

Part 8: Consequences

The air aboard the *Oregon* carried a weight that couldn't be measured, a tension that seemed to seep into every bolt, every panel, every breath. Despite the resolution of their immediate crisis, no one on board believed the danger was truly gone. It lingered in the back of every mind, unspoken but understood—a shadow that refused to lift.

Carter sat at her station, her eyes locked on the console. Data streams rolled across the screen, a cascade of numbers and symbols that only she seemed to decipher. Her focus was unwavering, but the faint crease between her brows betrayed her concern.

A soft ping broke the silence. Her fingers froze mid-typing, her pulse quickening as she leaned closer. "Captain," she said, her voice breaking the quiet with an urgency that sent ripples through the room.

King turned from his position at the central console, his gaze sharpening. "What is it?"

Carter didn't look up. "I'm picking up new signals—low frequency, faint, but distinct. They're not from *Sokol*. This is something else. Another vessel, likely Soviet."

The room seemed to hold its breath. Green, standing nearby, stepped closer, his expression hardening. "Another submarine?"

Carter nodded, her fingers flying across the keyboard. "Possibly, but it's not just one signal. I'm detecting layered patterns. This could mean a task force—a surface vessel coordinating with a second sub."

King's jaw tightened, his mind already working through the implications. A second submarine could spell disaster for their mission, especially in their current state. "Can you confirm their position?"

"Not precisely," Carter admitted, frustration creeping into her voice. "They're staying just outside active range, using passive sonar to avoid detection. But they're close—too close."

The captain's voice cut through the growing tension. "Green, adjust our course. Let's see if we can put some distance between us and whatever they're planning."

Green moved to comply, his hands steady on the controls despite the weight of the moment. "Adjusting to thirty degrees north by northeast. Depth: 420 meters."

Meanwhile, Landry's voice crackled through the comms. "Captain, the repairs are holding, but we're running on borrowed time. The systems can't take another hit like that last one."

King pressed the comms button. "Understood. Prioritize stability over speed. We need to be ready for whatever's coming."

In the dim light of the command center, the crew exchanged uneasy glances. The weight of the unknown pressed down on them all. Carter continued to monitor the signals, her focus unrelenting.

"It's like they're circling us," she muttered, more to herself than anyone else. "They know we're here. They're just waiting for us to make a mistake."

Green glanced over, his voice low. "Let's make sure we don't."

King stepped back, addressing the crew in a tone that was calm but carried the gravity of their situation. "We've made it through today because of your discipline and determination. But the fight isn't over. We're not just dealing with one enemy—we're in the middle of a coordinated effort to dismantle everything we stand for."

He paused, his eyes meeting those of his officers. "I need every one of you ready. No room for doubt, no room for hesitation. Whatever they throw at us next, we'll meet it head-on."

The crew straightened, their resolve evident despite the exhaustion etched into their faces.

As the *Oregon* adjusted its course, Carter's console emitted another soft ping. Her heart sank as she analyzed the data. The signals weren't fading—they were growing stronger, converging.

She turned to King, her voice steady despite the chill running through her. "Captain, they're closing in. This isn't random. They're coordinating."

King's expression darkened, his mind racing. "We don't have the luxury of waiting for their next move. Prepare the ship for silent running. Landry, I want every system optimized for efficiency. Carter, keep tracking those signals. I want to know where they are before they know where we are."

The *Oregon* descended deeper into the ocean's cold embrace, the vast, unyielding darkness pressing against its hull. Every creak, every subtle shift was magnified in the silence, a constant reminder of their fragility.

In the control room, the crew moved with a quiet efficiency, their actions precise and deliberate. Despite the tension, there was an unspoken unity among them, a shared determination to see this mission through.

King stood at the center of it all, his presence a steadying force. As he looked around at his crew, he felt a flicker of something beyond the immediate danger—a sense of pride in their resilience, their unwavering resolve.

"We've been underestimated before," he said quietly, more to himself than anyone else. "But not this time."

Part 1: A Risky Maneuver

The faint hum of the *Oregon's* systems vibrated through the hull like a second heartbeat, steady and unyielding. In the dimly lit control room, the crew moved with silent precision, their faces set with the grim determination of those who knew the stakes. Every sound, from the soft clicks of instruments to the whisper of shifting uniforms, seemed magnified in the pressurized silence.

Carter leaned over her console, her sharp eyes scanning the data streaming across the screen. The low-frequency signals she had been tracking for hours shifted ever so slightly, a subtle distortion that sent a chill down her spine. She pushed a stray strand of hair out of her face and activated the comm.

"Captain," she said, her voice steady despite the quickening pulse in her chest. "Soviet sonar activity is increasing. They're closing in. It's subtle, but their frequency patterns are shifting—they're adjusting for depth."

Captain King turned from his post, his piercing gaze locking onto hers. "How close are we to the edge of their range?"

Carter hesitated, recalculating. "Not close enough," she admitted. "We'll need to move, and soon."

Across the room, Green was hunched over a topographic display of the seabed, the glowing lines of undersea ridges and trenches casting faint shadows over his face. He traced a finger along a particularly jagged section of the map.

"We've got a way out," he said, more to himself than anyone else. "But it's going to be tight—real tight."

King crossed the room in two measured steps. "Explain."

Green straightened, tapping the map with the back of his stylus. "This trench system here. If we drop down to 410 meters and cut through this channel, we can use the undersea ridges as cover. Their sonar will scatter against the rock formations, but..." He paused, his expression darkening.

"But what?" King demanded.

Green glanced at him, his voice dropping. "The passage narrows to less than 20 meters at one point. If we miscalculate—just by a hair—we could snag the hull or worse."

In the engineering bay, Landry was already preparing for the maneuver. The room buzzed with quiet urgency as his team worked to optimize the *Oregon's* systems for silent running. Landry himself was crouched by a control panel, recalibrating the flow to the propulsion system to minimize noise.

He barked out instructions without looking up. "I want every system operating at minimal output. That means no sudden shifts, no spikes. If you so much as sneeze too loud, I'll hear it, and so will they."

A junior engineer, wide-eyed but determined, nodded as she tightened a valve. "Understood, sir."

Landry straightened, wiping his hands on a rag. He hit the comm to the control room. "Captain, we're as quiet as we're going to get. Just don't ask for a sprint; the systems won't handle it."

King nodded at the report, his mind racing. He turned back to Green. "How long to get through that channel?"

"Four minutes, maybe five," Green replied. "But we'll need to hold our course perfectly. No room for error."

King's gaze hardened. "We don't have a choice. Plot the course, and be ready to execute on my command."

Green gave a tight nod and turned back to the console, his fingers dancing over the controls as he entered the coordinates. Carter, meanwhile, monitored the ever-tightening grid of Soviet sonar pings.

"They're sweeping wider," she muttered under her breath. "We don't have much time."

The tension in the room was palpable as King addressed the crew. His voice was calm but carried the weight of the moment.

"Listen carefully. We're about to thread a needle blindfolded. This maneuver has to be precise. One mistake, and we're done. Stay sharp, stay focused, and trust your team."

The crew nodded in unison, their faces set with steely determination. Each knew their role, and each understood the stakes.

As the *Oregon* began its slow descent into the trench, the hull groaned softly under the increasing pressure. The sound was a haunting reminder of just how unforgiving the ocean could be. Carter's eyes flicked to her screen, watching as the Soviet signals danced dangerously close.

"Hold steady," King said, his voice cutting through the quiet like a blade.

In the shadows of the ocean, the *Oregon* moved with ghostly precision, each creak and shift of the hull a testament to the skill and resolve of its crew. They were running out of time, but they weren't out of options— not yet.

Part 2: The First Steps

The *Oregon* eased forward, her hull whispering through the depths as though she, too, feared making a sound. The faint glow of control panels bathed the command room in an eerie, almost ethereal light, casting shadows that flickered with every subtle movement. The crew was a symphony of silent precision—every station alive with focus, yet not a single word spoken louder than a whisper.

At the navigation console, Green's hands moved with the precision of a concert pianist, his eyes darting between the topographic display and the controls. His voice, though calm, carried the edge of intensity. "Depth at 408 meters. Holding steady. Adjusting trajectory by two degrees starboard to align with the ridge."

Captain King stood nearby, his eyes fixed on the central display, where the jagged lines of undersea formations loomed like teeth. The trench was their shield, but it was also a trap—one wrong move, and they would be torn apart.

"Ease her in," King murmured, his tone measured but firm.

Carter, seated at her station, was a sentinel of sound. Her fingers hovered over the controls, her ears attuned to the faint pings and hums of distant sonar. A new blip on her monitor made her breath hitch. "Captain," she said quietly, her voice cutting through the room like a scalpel, "sonar activity is increasing. They're sweeping wider. We have less than 200 meters before we're in their effective range."

King nodded, his face impassive, though the weight of the moment pressed heavily on his shoulders.
"Keep tracking. Green, adjust speed to one-sixth power. Let's keep our noise profile as low as possible."

"Aye, Captain," Green replied, his fingers adjusting the controls with a deftness born of countless hours of practice.

In the engineering bay, Landry monitored the propulsion systems with an almost predatory vigilance. His team moved efficiently around him, each member executing their tasks with the precision of a well-oiled machine. Landry's voice, though low, carried authority. "Pressure levels steady. No spikes in coolant flow. Keep it that way, people. We can't afford any surprises."

A younger engineer hesitated, glancing at a flickering gauge. "Sir, the auxiliary pump is—"

"I see it," Landry interrupted, his eyes narrowing as he adjusted a valve. "It's stable for now. Just keep an eye on it. If it wavers again, we shut it down manually. Got it?"

The engineer nodded, her face a mask of concentration.

Back in the control room, the tension was palpable. The *Oregon* edged closer to the narrowest part of the trench, the walls of rock pressing in on either side. Green's voice broke the silence.

"Approaching critical point. Passage narrows to 18 meters. Recommend reducing speed by another ten percent."

King glanced at Carter. "Sonar?"

"Still distant," she replied, though her brow furrowed. "But their range is closing. We're threading the needle, Captain."

"We always are," King said quietly, more to himself than anyone else.

The submarine slowed, her hull groaning softly under the strain of the maneuver. Every creak and groan seemed amplified in the silence, a haunting reminder of the immense pressure outside. Carter's eyes darted between her screens, watching for any changes in the enemy's pattern.

"Hold steady," King ordered, his voice a calm anchor in the storm of tension.

Green's hands tightened on the controls, guiding the *Oregon* with surgical precision through the treacherous path. The trench seemed to close in around them, the rocky walls visible even on the dim sonar imaging.

The crew worked in perfect unison, every movement purposeful and deliberate. In the stillness, the sound of their breathing was almost deafening. Even the faintest whisper carried weight, the unspoken acknowledgment of the danger they faced.

Carter's voice broke the silence once more.
"Captain, their sonar sweep just hit the edge of the trench. If they adjust their angle by even a degree, they'll find us."

King's jaw tightened. "Then let's make sure they don't."

The *Oregon* pressed forward, her crew braced for whatever lay ahead, each knowing that the slightest misstep could mean their end.

Part 3: Detection

The tense quiet of the *Oregon* shattered as Carter's console emitted a sharp, insistent ping. Her heart leapt into her throat, and her fingers flew over the controls, verifying the data with a sinking sense of dread. The room seemed to grow colder as she turned toward Captain King, her voice tight and controlled.

"Captain, we've been pinged. Direct sonar contact. They've found us."

For a split second, the control room froze, the weight of her words pressing down on everyone like the ocean above them. But King reacted instantly, his voice cutting through the stunned silence like a blade.

"Full speed, one-third power! Get us out of this trench, now!"

Green's hands flew to the controls, his jaw clenched as he brought the *Oregon* to life. The submarine surged forward, the engines humming with newfound urgency. In the tight confines of the trench, every movement felt perilously close to disaster.

Carter's eyes darted between her screens, tracking the enemy's movements.
"Their sonar is sweeping aggressively," she reported, her voice rising with the tension. "They're locking onto us. Captain, they're closing in!"

King gritted his teeth, his mind racing.
"Green, take us up to 390 meters and prepare for evasive maneuvers. Carter, give me a real-time update on their range."

"Range decreasing fast," Carter said, her hands shaking slightly as she worked. "They're only 400 meters behind us and closing."

The first torpedo launch came without warning. A distant, muffled thud reverberated through the water, followed by a rush of bubbles on Carter's monitor.
"They've fired!" she shouted, her voice cutting through the mounting chaos.

"Confirmed," Green said, his tone grim. "Torpedo inbound. Estimated impact in 30 seconds."

King's mind worked with lightning speed.

"Deploy countermeasures! Prepare for emergency dive on my mark!"

Landry's voice crackled over the comms from the engineering bay. "Captain, the systems are already running hot. If we push any harder—"

"Then we push," King interrupted, his voice hard as steel. "If we don't, there won't be an *Oregon* left to save."

The submarine shifted sharply as countermeasure canisters were deployed, releasing a cloud of noise and decoys meant to confuse the incoming torpedo. Green adjusted their trajectory, bringing the *Oregon* up and out of the trench, the narrow walls finally giving way to open water.

"Torpedo impact averted," Carter reported, relief flickering in her voice. But it was short-lived. "Another launch! Two torpedoes this time!"

"They're trying to box us in," Green muttered, his hands tightening on the controls. "Captain, we won't outrun them for long like this."

King's eyes swept the room, taking in the controlled chaos around him. The hum of the engines was louder now, a constant reminder of their peril. The *Oregon* was fast, but it wasn't built for prolonged sprints like this. They needed a way out.

"Carter, what's their formation?" King demanded.

She scanned the data, her voice steady despite the mounting tension. "They're coming in from two angles, coordinating fire. They're not just chasing us—they're herding us toward their fleet."

King's jaw tightened. "Then we don't let them."

The second volley of torpedoes closed in, their deadly hum vibrating through the hull. Green expertly maneuvered the submarine, banking hard to port and narrowly avoiding collision with a rocky outcropping. The *Oregon* dove deeper, its sleek form cutting through the water like a blade.

"Countermeasures deployed," Carter announced, her hands moving with practiced precision. "One torpedo diverted. Second is still tracking us!"

"Brace for impact!" King shouted, gripping the edge of his console.

The torpedo exploded just behind the *Oregon*, the shockwave slamming into the submarine and sending it lurching forward. Alarms blared, and the lights flickered momentarily, casting the control room into chaos. Landry's voice crackled through the comms, strained but clear. "Captain, we've sustained minor damage to the aft stabilizers. We're still operational, but any more hits like that—"

"I know," King cut him off, his voice sharper than ever. "Green, keep us moving. Carter, keep tracking their movements. We're not out of this yet."

The *Oregon* surged forward, her crew battered but undeterred. The chase was far from over, and the enemy was relentless. But even as the odds stacked against them, the crew moved with a singular purpose, their determination unshaken.

"We'll make it," King said quietly, almost to himself, his eyes locked on the screen. "We have to."

Part 4: The Depths of the Chase

The *Oregon* plunged deeper into the watery labyrinth, the undersea ridges and jagged rock formations looming like ancient sentinels in the murky dark. The submarine's sleek frame darted through narrow passages, a ghost fleeing from a relentless predator. The ocean was unforgiving—every sharp turn, every drop in depth brought the vessel perilously close to disaster.

"Depth at 430 meters," Green announced, his voice tight as his hands gripped the controls. Beads of sweat gathered at his temple, but his focus never wavered. "Approaching the ridge. Adjusting trajectory by three degrees portside."

The command center hummed with tense activity, each creak of the hull and whine of the engines a stark reminder of the pressure surrounding them. Carter's eyes never left her screen, where the relentless pings of the Soviet sonar painted a grim picture.

"Captain," she said, her voice low but firm. "Their sonar sweeps are tightening. They're moving to active pings again—they're narrowing down our position."

Captain King nodded, his face a mask of calm under fire. He stood at his post like a commander surveying a battlefield, his sharp gaze darting between Carter's data and the navigation display. "Keep tracking their patterns. I want to know the instant they adjust their depth or trajectory."

The *Oregon* banked hard to avoid a massive outcropping of rock, the maneuver sending a low groan reverberating through the hull. It was a sound that made even the seasoned crew wince—a stark reminder of the unforgiving environment they navigated.

"Careful, Green," King warned, though his tone remained steady.

Green didn't look up, his focus razor-sharp. "No room for error, sir. I've got this."

Carter glanced at him briefly, her expression a mixture of trust and tension. "Let's hope their sonar doesn't pick up that groan," she muttered.

In the engineering bay, Landry and his team worked with a frenetic precision that bordered on controlled chaos. The propulsion system groaned under the strain, its temperature gauges climbing dangerously high. Landry barked orders over the clatter of tools and the hiss of steam.

"Coolant flow is stabilizing, but she's running hot," he called into the comm. "Captain, we can maintain speed for another five minutes—maybe six—but we're walking a fine line here."

King's voice came through the speaker, firm and resolute. "Do what you can, Landry. We don't have a choice."

Landry scowled, adjusting a valve with practiced force. "We never do," he muttered under his breath, his hands moving to recalibrate the system for maximum efficiency.

Back in the control room, Carter's voice broke the tense quiet. "Sonar ping—directly ahead!"

King's eyes snapped to the navigation display.
"Green, adjust course! Take us down to 450 meters. Use the thermal layer to scatter their signals."

Green nodded, his hands dancing over the controls as he guided the *Oregon* deeper into the abyss. The submarine tilted slightly, her descent smooth but nerve-wracking.

"The ridge narrows ahead," Carter warned, her fingers tapping on her screen. "We'll need to thread the needle again."

King's jaw tightened. "We've done it before. We'll do it again. Green, keep us steady. Carter, track their movements. I want a full picture of their approach."

The Soviet sonar pings grew louder, sharper, their intervals shorter. The enemy was closing the gap, and every second felt like a lifetime. The tension in the control room was palpable, the air thick with unspoken fear and relentless determination.

"They're at 400 meters," Carter said, her voice barely audible over the hum of the systems. "Adjusting course—they're predicting our trajectory."

"They're good," Green muttered through gritted teeth. "But we're better."

The submarine weaved through the underwater maze with a precision that bordered on the miraculous. Each turn, each descent felt like a gamble against the odds, but the crew worked in perfect unison, their collective expertise a shield against the mounting danger.

The first glimpse of open water appeared on the sonar display—a faint promise of escape. But Carter's screen lit up with a new alarm.

"Captain," she said, her voice tense, "they're deploying torpedoes—two inbound!"

King reacted instantly.
"Deploy countermeasures! Green, evasive maneuvers—now!"

The *Oregon* lurched sharply to starboard, the sudden shift throwing several crew members off balance. A stream of decoy canisters burst from the submarine, releasing clouds of noise and thermal interference to confuse the approaching torpedoes.

"First torpedo diverted," Carter reported, her voice clipped but controlled. "Second is still tracking!"

King gripped the edge of his station, his mind racing. "Brace for impact!"

The shockwave from the torpedo's detonation slammed into the *Oregon*, shaking the vessel to its core. The lights flickered, and a few alarms blared momentarily before the systems recalibrated.

Landry's voice crackled over the comm. "Captain, we're still operational, but she's taking a beating. Stabilizers are holding—barely."

King exhaled sharply, his focus unbroken. "Green, get us out of this trench. Carter, keep tracking their sonar. We're not done yet."

The *Oregon* pressed on, her crew battered but resolute. The depths of the ocean held their fate, and the chase was far from over.

Part 5: A Radical Decision

The control room was a crucible of tension. The *Oregon* trembled as she navigated the relentless pursuit of the Soviet submarine. Captain King stood rigid, his gaze fixed on the sonar display where the enemy's pings encircled them like a predator closing in on its prey. The options were dwindling.

"Captain," Carter said, her voice steady but carrying an undercurrent of urgency. "We're nearing the limits of their sonar range, but their pings are narrowing in. If they adjust by even a fraction, they'll have us locked."

King's eyes hardened, his jaw set with steely determination. "Then we'll make sure they don't. Prepare to descend—450 meters won't cut it. We're going deeper."

A ripple of surprise swept through the crew. Green turned to King, his brow furrowed. "Deeper, sir? At this speed, with the damage we've sustained, we're already pushing it."

King didn't flinch. "We go deeper, Mr. Green. They won't follow us into the abyss. Plot the trajectory and ensure we keep the strain on the stabilizers balanced."

Carter's fingers flew over her console, her voice cutting through the rising tension.
"Captain, with all due respect, the hull is already under immense pressure. If we push past 600 meters—"

"We push," King interrupted, his voice low and resolute. "We either take the risk or let them pin us down. That's not an option."

Carter hesitated, then gave a curt nod, her hands resuming their rapid calculations.

In the engineering bay, Landry stared at the blinking gauges with grim focus. The readings were creeping into dangerous territory, the hull groaning audibly under the strain. His team moved like clockwork, their faces tight with concentration.

"Captain," Landry's voice crackled over the comms, "you're asking for a miracle here. The stabilizers are holding, but not by much. You sure you want to roll these dice?"

"I'm sure," King replied without hesitation. "Redirect all auxiliary power to the key systems. We need every ounce of stability for this descent."

Landry exhaled sharply, muttering to himself. "You heard the man! Let's make the impossible happen. Again."

His team sprang into action, adjusting valves, monitoring pressure levels, and rerouting power with precision born of necessity.

Green's hands moved deftly across the controls, his jaw tight with concentration. "Adjusting trajectory. Angle set at three degrees. Depth estimate: 580 meters. Captain, we'll be riding the edge."

"That's where we live," King said calmly, gripping the edge of his console. "Begin descent."

The *Oregon* tilted downward, her sleek frame cutting through the depths with relentless purpose. The hull groaned under the mounting pressure, the sound reverberating through the control room like the mournful cry of a leviathan.

Carter's voice broke through the tense silence.
"Their sonar's range is fragmenting, but they're adapting. We're still within their sweep."

"Not for long," King replied, his voice firm. "We'll force them to choose—follow us and risk their own hulls or let us go."

The submarine descended further, the ambient light outside fading into inky blackness. The oppressive weight of the ocean pressed against them, a silent reminder of the dangers they faced.

In the engineering bay, Landry barked orders over the rising hum of the systems. "Coolant flow stable! Pressure levels approaching critical, but holding!"

One of the junior engineers glanced at him nervously. "Sir, the aft stabilizer is fluctuating—"

"I see it," Landry snapped, his hands moving to adjust the controls. "Rebalance the load. We're not giving this thing an inch."

The *Oregon* reached the target depth, the hull groaning louder than ever. Carter's screen flickered with data as she analyzed the enemy's signals. "Captain, their sonar is fragmenting completely. The thermal layers are scattering their pings. They're losing us."

A faint smile flickered across King's lips, but it didn't reach his eyes. "Hold steady. Let's see if they have the stomach to follow us."

The minutes stretched into eternity as the crew waited, their breaths shallow and their eyes glued to their stations. Then, Carter spoke, her voice carrying a note of relief.

"They're changing course. Pulling back to shallower waters."

A wave of quiet relief swept through the control room, but King's expression remained unreadable.

"Good work, everyone. Landry, report."

Landry's voice came through, laced with exhaustion. "Hull integrity is stable for now, but she's been through hell, Captain. We'll need to surface soon for any real repairs."

"Understood," King replied. "Green, hold position and prepare for ascent. Carter, confirm their withdrawal."

The *Oregon* hung suspended in the crushing depths, her crew battered but alive. They had survived another impossible challenge, but the strain was evident in every creak of the hull and every line on their faces.

King's voice broke the heavy silence. "This isn't over. They'll regroup, and we'll be ready. But for now, take a moment—each of you. You've earned it."

The crew exchanged weary glances, a flicker of pride breaking through the tension. They had defied the odds once again, but the battle was far from over.

Part 6: Depth of Despair

The *Oregon* dove into the abyss, the faint glow of its control panels the only light in a world of inky blackness. The submarine groaned under the crushing weight of the ocean above, each metallic creak and moan a haunting reminder of how fragile they were in this hostile environment. The crew held their breath collectively, a silent prayer to the steel walls around them, begging them to hold.

Carter's fingers trembled slightly as she monitored the sonar, her screen awash with fractured pings and scattered signals. The once-clear sound of the enemy sonar was now distorted, broken by the thermal layers and the oppressive depths.

"Captain," she whispered, her voice barely audible over the tense hum of the control room, "their signals are faltering. We're slipping out of their reach."

King stood like a statue, his hands gripping the edge of his console, knuckles white. His gaze remained fixed on the displays, his jaw set in determination. "Good," he said evenly. "But we're not out of this yet. Keep monitoring their patterns."

The hull let out a long, eerie groan, a sound that sent shivers through the spine of even the most seasoned sailors. Green's hands danced across the controls, guiding the submarine with the precision of a surgeon.

"Depth: 610 meters," Green announced, his voice strained but steady. "Holding course. Any deeper, and we're gambling with the hull."

"Let's not gamble any more than we have to," King replied, his tone measured, though his heart pounded in his chest. "Ease her into the thermal layer. We move slowly and steadily."

Green nodded, his focus unshakable, but the tension in his shoulders was visible. Each adjustment he made was precise, calculated to the millimeter. The submarine's engines hummed softly, a whisper against the crushing silence of the deep.

In the engineering bay, Landry's team worked with frantic efficiency, sweat dripping down their faces as they monitored the systems. Gauges flirted with the red zones, and the constant creaks of the hull were a grim backdrop to their efforts.

"Coolant levels holding," Landry barked, his voice cutting through the chaos. "But she's feeling the strain. Stabilizers are at their limit."

One of the junior engineers looked up from his console, his face pale. "Sir, if we take another shift in pressure—"

"We won't," Landry snapped, though his hands moved with extra care as he fine-tuned the systems. "Keep the flow steady. The captain's counting on us, and I'm not about to let him down."

Back in the control room, Carter's voice broke the silence again. "Captain, their sonar sweeps are scattering. The thermal layer is interfering with their signals."

King's lips tightened into the faintest semblance of a smile. "Let's keep it that way. Green, bring us to 620 meters, no more. I want us deep enough to stay hidden but not so far that we risk structural failure."

The submarine descended further, the pressure outside mounting with every meter. The creaks of the hull grew louder, a metallic symphony of stress that reverberated through the vessel. The air in the control room was thick with tension, every crew member hyper-aware of the stakes.

Carter kept her eyes glued to her screen, her voice breaking the silence in sharp bursts. "Signals weakening. They're losing us... almost out of range now."

Green adjusted the controls with the precision of a concert pianist, his jaw clenched as he guided the submarine through the unseen maze below. "Almost there," he murmured, more to himself than anyone else.

The submarine leveled out at 620 meters, her frame groaning in protest but holding firm. The control room was deathly quiet, the crew waiting with bated breath to see if the maneuver had worked.

Minutes passed like hours, each second a test of their resolve. Finally, Carter looked up, a flicker of relief in her eyes.
"They're retreating. Their sonar sweeps are moving back to shallower depths. We're clear, Captain."

A collective exhale swept through the control room, the tension breaking like a wave. King's shoulders relaxed fractionally, though his eyes remained sharp.

"Well done, everyone," he said, his voice calm but carrying the weight of hard-won relief. "Green, hold us here. Landry, status on the hull?"

Landry's voice came through the intercom, weary but steady. "She's holding, Captain. Barely, but she's holding. Recommend we stay steady until we're sure they're out of range."

"Noted," King replied. "Carter, keep tracking their movements. I don't want any surprises."

The *Oregon* hung in the dark silence of the deep, her crew battered but alive. They had survived the impossible once again, but the weight of the ordeal was etched into every face, every line of their tense bodies.

"Take a moment," King said, his voice softer now. "We'll surface when it's safe, but for now, breathe. You've earned it."

The crew exchanged weary glances, a flicker of pride breaking through their exhaustion. They were still in the fight, and though the battle was far from over, they had proven their resilience once more.

Part 7: A Temporary Respite

The *Oregon* lay suspended in the abyss, the echoes of its desperate escape still vibrating through the steel hull. The control room was quieter now, the frenzied urgency replaced with a heavy stillness as the crew processed what they had just endured. Each face reflected a mixture of relief and exhaustion, though no one dared let their guard down entirely.

Carter's voice broke the silence, steady but cautious.
"Captain, their sonar signals are retreating. They've moved to shallower waters and are adjusting their search patterns. For now, we're out of range."

A wave of restrained relief rippled through the control room. Green leaned back in his chair slightly, exhaling a breath he didn't realize he'd been holding.
"That's the best news I've heard all day," he muttered, wiping sweat from his brow.

King remained at his station, his hands still gripping the edge of the console. Though his posture was calm, his eyes scanned the room, taking in the subdued tension that lingered among his crew. Finally, he spoke, his voice firm but carrying an undercurrent of gratitude.

"Well done, all of you. We've pushed this boat and ourselves to the limit, and you've proven once again why this crew is the best there is. Take a moment to catch your breath. We're not out of this yet, but you've earned this pause."

The crew exchanged quiet, tired smiles. It wasn't a victory celebration, but it was something—a shared acknowledgment of their resilience.

In the engineering bay, Landry leaned heavily against a console, his team scattered around him in various states of exhaustion. The systems still hummed, though the readings on the displays were far from comforting. "Cooling's holding steady," Landry reported through the intercom. "But the stabilizers are on their last legs, Captain. We've got micro-fractures in a couple of the seals, and the pressure gauges aren't exactly making me feel warm and fuzzy."

"Can we hold our position?" King's voice came through, calm but with the weight of unspoken urgency.

"For now," Landry replied. "But if they get wind of us again, we won't be pulling stunts like that twice."

Carter glanced at her monitors, her sharp eyes catching every shift in the data.
"Their search grid is expanding," she said, addressing the room. "They're covering more area now, but they're keeping to the mid-depths. I don't think they're willing to risk following us this far down."

King nodded, his mind already moving to the next steps. "Good. Let's keep it that way. Maintain current depth and course for now, but stay sharp. This isn't over."

Green turned to him, his expression a mix of relief and curiosity. "What's the play here, Captain? Do we wait them out or make a break for it?"

King's gaze was steady as he replied.
"We wait. They'll tire eventually, but we're not giving them any reason to think we're still here. For now, our best weapon is patience."

The control room settled into a quieter rhythm, though the tension remained palpable. Every creak of the hull, every faint beep of the consoles seemed amplified in the silence.

Green adjusted the trajectory slightly, his movements precise despite the exhaustion evident in his face.

"I'll keep us steady," he said, mostly to himself. "No more surprises on my watch."

Carter's focus remained on her displays, her analytical mind still working at full speed.

"If they shift their search pattern again, we'll have to be ready. The moment we see an opening, we need to act."

King allowed himself a brief moment to look around the room, at the faces of his crew. They were exhausted, battered by the ordeal, but their professionalism and determination shone through.

Finally, King addressed the crew, his voice carrying the weight of both their recent ordeal and the challenges ahead.

"You've all done exceptional work today. This mission has tested us in ways we couldn't have anticipated, but we've held our own. Remember that."

He paused, letting the words settle.

"But we're not done. The enemy is still out there, and the stakes haven't changed. Take this moment to regroup and recharge, because the next move will be just as critical as the last."

The crew nodded silently, their expressions resolute. They knew the road ahead was far from easy, but they also knew they could rely on each other—and their captain.

In the cold depths of the ocean, the *Oregon* remained a shadow in the dark, her crew united by the trials they had faced and the battles still to come. Though the moment was fleeting, the sense of quiet triumph was enough to carry them forward.

Part 8: The Final Order

The dim glow of the control room lights reflected on the weary faces of the crew. The *Oregon* floated silently in the crushing depths, temporarily safe but far from secure. Every member of the team knew the reprieve they'd earned was fragile at best, a fleeting moment before the storm would inevitably resume.

Captain King stood at his post, his gaze fixed on the central display. The enemy's sonar signals were a faint echo now, their grid sweeping far above and away. But King's expression was grim; he knew this was no victory, only a delay in the inevitable clash.

"Carter," King said, his voice steady but laced with steel, "confirm the enemy's movements."

Carter's fingers danced over her console, the soft hum of the equipment the only sound in the room.
"They've pulled back, Captain. Their grid is expanding toward the northeast, but they're maintaining presence near the edge of our current position. They're not giving up."

King nodded slowly, his expression unreadable.
"They won't. Not until they've exhausted every option—or we give them a reason to stop looking. Green," he turned to his helmsman, "set a course due west, bearing 270. Prepare for silent running. We're moving to the next phase."

Green straightened in his seat, his hands instinctively adjusting the controls. His voice was calm, but the tension in his posture was evident. "Course set, Captain. Adjusting speed for minimal acoustic signature."

The submarine shifted smoothly, its sleek body cutting through the dark waters with an almost imperceptible motion. The creaks and groans of the hull, though quieter now, were a constant reminder of the depths pressing down upon them.

King turned back to address the room, his voice carrying the weight of authority and the hard-earned respect of his crew. "This was only the beginning. We've bought ourselves time, but the enemy knows we're here. They're not going to stop until they find us— or until we complete this mission. What happens next will define whether we come out of this intact."

The crew listened in silence, their exhaustion momentarily overshadowed by the determination in King's tone.

"Landry," King continued, "what's the status of the systems?"

The voice of the chief engineer came through the comms, steady but tinged with fatigue.
"She's holding, Captain, but she's hurting. Stabilizers are stable for now, and I've rerouted auxiliary power to reinforce the critical systems. We can push if we need to, but I wouldn't recommend another stunt like that one anytime soon."

King acknowledged the report with a curt nod. "Understood. Keep monitoring and report any changes immediately."

Carter glanced at her monitors, her sharp eyes catching every flicker of data.
"We're clear for now, but their fleet's movements suggest they're regrouping. They're not done with us yet."

"No, they're not," King said quietly. He turned to the crew, his gaze sweeping across the room. "And neither are we. This mission isn't about survival—it's about success. We have a job to do, and we're going to finish it."

There was no applause, no cheers—just the quiet determination of seasoned sailors who knew the stakes. Each of them had been tested, and each had proven their worth.

As the *Oregon* began its westward journey, the crew settled into their stations, the tension in the room easing but never fully dissipating. They moved with the efficiency of a machine, every action deliberate and precise.

Green kept his focus on the controls, his hands steady despite the weight of the past hours.
"Course holding steady. If we maintain this trajectory, we'll be clear of their immediate range within the hour."

"Good," King replied, his tone softer now. "Let's keep it that way."

Carter glanced at him, her expression thoughtful.
"Captain, what if they anticipate our move? If they predict our heading, we might run straight into their reinforcements."

King's lips pressed into a thin line.

"Then we'll do what we always do—adapt. But for now, we stick to the plan. We can't afford to second-guess ourselves at every turn."

The ocean stretched endlessly around them, a vast, silent void that both protected and threatened them in equal measure. The crew of the *Oregon* knew they were far from safe, but they also knew they had each other— and their captain—to guide them through the darkness.

King allowed himself a brief moment to breathe, his hands resting on the edge of the console. His voice, when he spoke again, was quieter but no less resolute.

"Stay sharp. This isn't over. It's only just begun."

The *Oregon* moved forward into the unknown, her crew braced for whatever lay ahead. The mission was far from over, and the challenges they had faced were only the prelude to the battles yet to come.

Chapter 9: Crossing the Line

Part 1: Beneath the Cover of Darkness

The *Oregon* moved like a shadow, her engines throttled to a whisper as she slid through the labyrinth of underwater ridges. The cold, dark waters seemed to press in from all sides, an oppressive blanket of silence broken only by the occasional creak of the hull. Inside, the atmosphere was just as tense. The crew worked with laser focus, their movements precise, their voices hushed to a whisper. Every action felt like walking a tightrope, each second an exercise in restraint.

At her station, Carter hunched over her console, the faint glow of the screen casting sharp shadows on her determined face. Her fingers flew across the controls, recalibrating sensors and scanning for the faintest echoes of enemy sonar.

"They're pulling back," she murmured, her voice soft but firm. "But not far. They're sweeping the area to the north, still close enough to pick us up if we're careless."

King, standing near the center of the room, didn't respond immediately. His gaze swept over the crew, assessing their state. Exhaustion was evident in their eyes, but so was focus.

"Stay steady," he said finally, his voice calm but edged with authority. "We're not out of this yet. Green, keep her tight to the rift. I don't want us exposed for even a second."

Green, seated at the helm, nodded without looking up. His hands were steady on the controls, but a bead of sweat ran down his temple, betraying the strain of the precision required.
"Rift's narrowing ahead," he reported. "We've got about twenty meters clearance on either side. Should be enough, but we'll need to ease her through."

"Do it," King replied simply.

The submarine shifted slightly, its sleek frame slipping deeper into the natural trench. The walls of the underwater ridge loomed close, their jagged edges threatening to scrape the hull with even the smallest error.

The hull groaned faintly as the pressure increased, and a faint tremor ran through the deck. Green's jaw tightened, but his hands never wavered.

Carter glanced over her shoulder.
"Captain, we're nearing the outer boundary of their last detected sweep. If we can stay hidden for the next ten minutes, we'll clear the immediate zone."

"Understood," King said. His gaze remained fixed on the displays, every muscle in his body radiating tension.

From her station, Carter leaned back slightly, her mind racing through the possibilities.
"Captain," she said after a pause, "there's a current up ahead—weak, but steady. If we ride it, it could help mask our movements. It's not on their direct path."

King turned his sharp gaze toward her.
"Explain."

"It's a natural current," she continued, pointing to her screen. "It moves westward, away from their grid. If we position ourselves correctly, it might give us just enough cover to slip past without drawing attention."

Green glanced over, his interest piqued.
"She's right," he said, adjusting the helm slightly to align with Carter's suggestion. "But we'll need to hit the current at the perfect angle, or we risk overexposing ourselves."

King considered for a brief moment before nodding. "Do it. Carter, guide him in. Green, you know what to do."

The tension in the room thickened as the crew worked in unison. Carter called out adjustments while Green fine-tuned their trajectory. Every movement of the submarine felt deliberate, as if the *Oregon* herself was holding her breath.

The current caught the submarine gently, like an unseen hand guiding her forward. The shift was almost imperceptible, but the sonar readings on Carter's screen confirmed it: their noise signature had dropped even further.

"Current's carrying us," Carter said quietly. "We're in the sweet spot."

For several agonizing minutes, the *Oregon* drifted in near silence. The crew watched their stations intently, each person hyper-aware of the stakes. Finally, Carter's voice broke the silence again, this time with a faint note of relief.

"They've shifted north. Their pings are moving away from us. We're clear for now."

A collective exhale swept through the room, though no one dared to fully relax. King allowed himself a small nod of approval.

"Good work," he said. "Green, bring us up slowly. Let's test the waters at a safer depth."

The submarine began a cautious ascent, each meter feeling like a mile as the crew monitored every creak and groan of the hull. The ocean remained dark and silent around them, but the faint glimmers of safety began to appear on the edges of their minds.

For now, they were invisible—hidden beneath the cover of darkness and the vastness of the ocean. But every person aboard knew this was only the beginning of the final stretch.

Part 2: The Final Threat

The faint hum of machinery filled the *Oregon*'s control room, the only sound in an otherwise suffocating silence. The submarine drifted on the edge of a fragile escape, her crew locked in a delicate dance with the ocean and the invisible enemy above. But that silence shattered when Carter's console emitted a sharp ping.

"Captain," she said, her voice low but urgent. "New contacts. Multiple signals from the north-northeast."

King turned to her, his gaze cutting through the dim light of the room. "What kind of signals?"

She adjusted the dials, the glowing lines on her screen shifting as she filtered out noise. Her face tightened.
"Hydroacoustic sweeps—broad and deliberate. They're sending out a new search pattern. And…" Her voice faltered as she zoomed in on one particular signal. "There's something airborne. Could be a patrol aircraft dropping sonobuoys."

The room tensed at her words. A patrol aircraft meant the enemy wasn't just guessing anymore—they were actively hunting.

King straightened, his presence commanding calm amid the rising tension.
"Options?"

Green, his hands still steady on the helm, spoke without turning his head. "We could dive deeper, but the ridges are too tight. Too much movement and we'll scrape the hull."

Carter chimed in, her tone clipped.
"If they deploy more sonobuoys, staying stationary won't help. They'll narrow down our position in minutes."

The weight of her statement settled over the room. The enemy was closing in, and time was running out.

King's mind worked quickly, calculating risks and outcomes. His eyes flicked to the engineering console.
"Landry, what can you rig to throw them off?"

In the engineering bay, Landry was already moving, his team scattering to gather tools and components.
"We could try a noise maker," he said through the intercom, his voice crackling slightly. "Something to mimic another vessel—close enough to draw their attention, but far enough not to compromise us."

King nodded. "Make it happen. And fast."

Landry didn't need further instruction. His hands moved with practiced efficiency as he pieced together an improvised device—a combination of spare parts and sheer ingenuity. He barked orders to his team, their movements synchronized like clockwork despite the urgency.

"Captain," Landry's voice came through the comm again, "device ready. I can deploy it within a minute, but you'll need to adjust course to make it convincing."

Back in the control room, Green's fingers danced across the controls, preparing to shift the submarine's heading.
"Ready when you are, Captain," he said.

"Do it," King ordered. "Carter, monitor their response. I want to know the second they take the bait."

The *Oregon* shifted slightly, her sleek form gliding into a new position as Landry's team launched the decoy. The device sank into the depths, its mechanisms springing to life. Within moments, it began emitting a series of calculated pings—perfectly mimicking the signature of a smaller submarine.

Carter watched her screen intently, her sharp eyes tracking the enemy signals.
"They're reacting," she said, her voice tinged with both relief and tension. "Their pattern's changing. The airborne unit is shifting north— toward the decoy."

The room remained silent, save for the faint hum of the sonar. Each second felt like an eternity as the crew waited to see if the ploy would hold. Finally, Carter leaned back slightly, exhaling a breath she didn't realize she'd been holding.
"They've taken the bait. Their sweeps are moving away from us."

King allowed himself a brief nod.
"Green, adjust our heading. Let's put as much distance as we can between us and that mess."

Green complied, guiding the submarine further into the safety of the underwater ridge. The *Oregon* moved like a ghost, her engines barely audible as she slipped through the dark waters.

In the engineering bay, Landry leaned against a console, wiping sweat from his brow. His team exchanged weary glances, the tension of the moment finally beginning to ease.

"Nice work," one of the junior engineers muttered.

"Don't celebrate yet," Landry replied, though a faint smile tugged at the corners of his mouth. "We're not out of the woods."

Back in the control room, King's voice cut through the low murmur. "Status?"

Carter's hands moved over the console, her focus unbroken. "Signals are dispersing. They've committed to the decoy. We're clear— for now."

King's gaze swept over the room, his crew still at their stations, their focus unwavering despite the exhaustion etched into their faces.

"Good work," he said firmly. "But stay sharp. They'll figure it out eventually, and we need to be long gone by the time they do."

The crew nodded silently, their resolve unbroken. The *Oregon* continued her silent run, slipping further from danger with every passing minute.

For now, they had bought themselves time. But they all knew the game wasn't over.

Part 3: The Breakthrough

The faint light of dawn filtered through the depths, turning the dark ocean a murky gray as the *Oregon* edged closer to international waters. The tension in the control room was palpable, each creak of the hull, every hum of the systems amplified by the silence. The crew worked with a single-minded focus, knowing that the end was near but refusing to relax until they were truly clear.

Carter leaned into her console, her eyes scanning the data feeds with the precision of a hawk. The sonar display was quiet now—blessedly quiet. The enemy signals that had haunted them for hours were nothing more than faint whispers, retreating into the void. Still, she double-checked every reading, unwilling to trust the reprieve until it was confirmed.

"Captain," she said finally, her voice steady but softer now, "we're past the boundary. All signals indicate they've halted pursuit." She glanced over her shoulder, meeting King's gaze. "We're in international waters."

A ripple of relief swept through the control room, subtle but unmistakable. A few shoulders dropped, breaths were exhaled quietly, and even the normally stoic Green allowed himself the ghost of a smile as he adjusted their heading.

King stood tall near the central console, his hands resting lightly on its edge. His expression remained composed, but there was a faint shift in his posture—a quiet acknowledgment of the victory they had just achieved.

"Maintain course," he ordered, his voice calm but firm. "Carter, confirm all systems are secure. Green, keep her steady."

As the crew moved to carry out his commands, the atmosphere in the room softened slightly. The weight of the mission, the fear and adrenaline that had fueled them, began to give way to something else—pride.

In the engineering bay, Landry leaned against a console, his team exchanging tired but triumphant glances. The engines, though battered, continued their steady hum, a testament to their skill and resilience.

"She held together," Landry muttered, patting a nearby panel as if the submarine could hear him. "Not bad for an old girl."

He keyed the comm, his voice carrying a rare note of levity. "Captain, propulsion systems are stable. Looks like we'll make it home without any more surprises—assuming you don't have any wild ideas for detours."

Back in the control room, Carter's fingers moved deftly over her console, running one final check. When she spoke again, her tone was lighter, almost warm.
"Data secure. Transmission complete. The mission's a success."

The words hung in the air for a moment, sinking in. The *Oregon* had done it. Against the odds, against the relentless pursuit of a superior force, they had completed their mission and lived to tell the tale.

King allowed himself a brief moment to look around the room, his gaze sweeping over his crew. Each face bore the marks of exhaustion—dark circles under their eyes, strained expressions—but there was something else now: a spark of pride, a sense of accomplishment that couldn't be dimmed.

"You've done exceptional work," King said, his voice carrying the weight of their shared experience. "Every one of you. This wasn't just a mission—it was a test of who we are, and you proved it."

His words were met with quiet nods and faint smiles. It wasn't in their nature to celebrate loudly, but the unspoken camaraderie filled the room like a tangible force.

As the submarine continued its glide through the open waters, the tension ebbed away completely, replaced by a solemn satisfaction. For the first time in days, the crew allowed themselves to believe they were safe.

Green broke the silence, his voice steady but tinged with dry humor. "Steady course, Captain. And just for the record, I wouldn't mind if the next mission came with a little less drama."

A few chuckles rippled through the room, lightening the mood further. Even King allowed himself a faint smirk.

The *Oregon* pressed onward, her scars a silent testament to the trials she and her crew had endured. Though battered, she moved with the grace of a ship that had earned her place in history. The horizon ahead was open and boundless, a promise of home just beyond sight.

King stood quietly at his station, watching the displays with a steady gaze. For all his composure, there was a deep well of pride within him—pride for his crew, for their resilience, and for their unyielding determination.

"Take us home," he said softly, his voice carrying a rare note of emotion.

And so the *Oregon* sailed on, leaving behind the shadows of the enemy and moving into the light of the open sea.

Part 4: A Wave of Relief

The *Oregon* glided through the vast expanse of open water, her engines humming steadily. The crushing tension of the last few days had finally begun to lift, leaving a charged silence in its wake. For the first time since their mission began, the crew felt the faint glimmer of safety on the horizon.

Carter sat at her console, her fingers deftly moving across the controls. The faint sonar echoes that had plagued them for so long had vanished entirely, leaving the screens blessedly empty. She took a moment to double-check, her sharp eyes ensuring no stray signal was missed. Finally, she leaned back, exhaling deeply.

"Captain," she said, turning slightly toward King, her voice steady but tinged with quiet satisfaction, "all signals indicate a full retreat. Soviet assets are no longer in range."

King stood near the central console, his stance relaxed but commanding. He absorbed her words in silence, his gaze fixed on the displays before him. After a long moment, he nodded, a small but genuine acknowledgment of their achievement.

"Good," he said simply. "Green, maintain course and speed. Let's keep things smooth."

In the engineering bay, Landry wiped his hands on a grease-stained rag, surveying the humming machinery around him. The battered systems that had been pushed to their limits were holding steady, a testament to his team's skill and perseverance. He keyed the intercom, his voice carrying a rare note of levity.

"Captain, temporary repairs are holding strong. No new warnings, no red lights. She's stable." He paused, then added with a smirk, "Feels like she's as ready for a break as we are."

King's voice came through the speaker, calm and steady as always. "Understood, Landry. Good work. Keep monitoring, but take a moment to catch your breath. You've earned it."

Landry chuckled softly, shaking his head as he turned back to his team. "You heard the man. But don't get too comfortable—we're not home yet."

Back in the control room, the soft chime of an incoming transmission broke the quiet. Carter immediately leaned forward, her fingers dancing across the console as she decrypted the message. The words appeared on the screen, brief but clear: *Mission success confirmed. Return to base.*

For a moment, the room was silent as the weight of the message sank in. Then a wave of quiet relief swept through the crew. Shoulders relaxed, breaths were exhaled, and even the faintest smiles began to appear on weary faces.

Carter turned to King, her eyes reflecting both exhaustion and pride. "Confirmation received, Captain. Mission is officially a success."

King allowed himself a rare moment of reflection, his gaze sweeping over the room. Each member of the crew bore the marks of the ordeal—dark circles under their eyes, tense postures—but in their expressions, he saw the strength and resolve that had carried them through.

"You've all earned this," he said, his voice carrying just enough warmth to soften the usual edge. "Take a moment. But remember, we're not home yet."

Green shifted in his seat, the faintest hint of a grin tugging at the corner of his mouth.
"Steady course set, Captain. And for the record, it feels good to be the ones delivering the message for a change."

A ripple of quiet laughter moved through the room, lightening the mood further. Even King allowed himself a faint smile before returning his focus to the displays.

The *Oregon* continued her journey, her damaged but resilient frame cutting through the open ocean with the grace of a ship that had earned her survival. The silence that had once been filled with tension now carried an air of calm, the crew allowing themselves to exhale for the first time in days.

Landry's voice came over the intercom again, breaking the quiet. "All systems stable. No issues to report. Feels strange to say, but… I think we're in the clear."

King glanced toward Carter, who nodded in agreement. "They've moved beyond detection range," she confirmed. "We're officially alone out here."

The words brought an almost palpable sense of relief to the room. For the first time, it felt like they could truly believe they were safe.

King straightened, his hands resting lightly on the console as he addressed the crew.
"You've done exceptional work. I know you're tired, and I know this hasn't been easy. But what you've accomplished here matters. It matters to us, and it matters to those who sent us out here."

His words were met with quiet nods and faint smiles. There were no cheers or grand displays of emotion—this was a crew that understood the weight of their work. But the sense of pride and camaraderie in the room was unmistakable.

As the submarine pressed onward toward the horizon, the open water stretched before them like a promise. The mission was complete, and the first steps toward home had begun.

The crew, though exhausted, carried with them the satisfaction of a job well done. The journey wasn't over, but for now, they allowed themselves to savor the quiet triumph.

The *Oregon* moved forward, her scars a testament to her resilience, her crew united in the knowledge that together, they had faced the unthinkable—and prevailed.

Part 1: The Final Miles

The *Oregon* broke through the surface of the ocean with a deliberate, almost reluctant groan. Her battered hull gleamed faintly under the weak morning light, the scars of her ordeal visible even beneath the shifting waves. The cold, gray sky stretched endlessly above, streaked with faint slivers of pink from the rising sun. It was a solemn, muted dawn—one that seemed to echo the mood of the crew within.

Green's hands gripped the helm tightly as he guided the submarine through her final maneuvers. Every movement was deliberate, every adjustment a calculated effort to preserve the fragile stability of their vessel. His face was lined with exhaustion, his eyes heavy, but there was a glint of pride that hadn't been there days ago. He had brought her this far, and he would see her safely home.

"We're clear," he announced softly, his voice breaking the heavy silence in the control room. "Final heading locked. No threats detected."

At her station, Carter leaned forward, her sharp eyes scanning the final readings on her console. The screens displayed nothing but the faint hum of open ocean. The last traces of Soviet signals had disappeared entirely, leaving only the rhythmic pulse of their own systems. She exhaled slowly, the tension in her shoulders easing for the first time in hours.

"Captain," she said, turning slightly toward King. "No sign of pursuit. We're alone out here."

King stood near the periscope, his tall frame silhouetted against the dim light filtering into the room. His posture remained commanding, but there was a subtle relaxation in his shoulders—a small acknowledgment of the words he'd just heard.

"Good," he said evenly, his voice carrying the same quiet authority that had steered them through so much. "Green, keep us steady. Carter, maintain passive monitoring until we're within visual range of the base."

In the engineering bay, Landry wiped his oil-streaked hands on a rag, his gaze fixed on a row of flickering indicators. The engines hummed steadily, though there were faint groans and creaks that spoke of the strain they had endured. He let out a low whistle, shaking his head as he leaned closer to inspect one of the panels.

"She's held together, but I wouldn't bet on another miracle," he muttered to himself. He reached for the intercom and pressed the button. "Captain, systems are holding stable for now. Propulsion's steady, but we're running on grit and duct tape. Let's not push her any harder than we have to."

King's response came back through the speaker, calm and unshakable. "Understood, Landry. Just get her to the dock."

Landry chuckled dryly, patting the console beside him.
"She'll make it. She's tougher than she looks."

The crew moved quietly through the submarine, their steps slow but steady. They were exhausted, their bodies and minds pushed to the brink, but there was a quiet resilience in their movements—a determination to see the mission through to its end.

As the submarine glided toward her destination, the first faint outlines of land appeared on the horizon. The sight brought a ripple of subdued emotion through the control room. For all their professionalism and training, they were human, and the sight of home was a balm to their battered spirits.

Green glanced toward King, a faint smile tugging at the corners of his lips.
"Not much farther now, Captain."

King gave a slight nod, his gaze fixed on the horizon.
"No," he said quietly. "Not much farther at all."

The gray waves lapped gently against the submarine's hull as she pushed forward, each movement precise and deliberate. The open sea stretched out around her, vast and unyielding, but the distant shore offered a glimmer of hope.

For the crew of the *Oregon*, this was more than just a return—it was survival. It was the culmination of days spent on the edge, fighting against impossible odds. And yet, even as they neared safety, the weight of their experiences lingered. The mission had been a success, but its cost was written in every scar on their vessel and every line etched into their faces.

As the submarine drew closer to the base, the mood in the control room shifted subtly. The tension hadn't disappeared entirely, but it had eased, replaced by a sense of quiet accomplishment. They had made it.

King stood silently for a moment, his hands resting lightly on the console. His gaze swept over his crew—Green at the helm, Carter at her station, the others working steadily despite their exhaustion.

"You've done well," he said finally, his voice carrying a rare warmth. "Take it in. You've earned it."

The crew exchanged brief glances, their expressions softening. There were no cheers, no loud celebrations. They were too tired for that. But in their quiet nods and faint smiles, there was an unspoken understanding— they had faced the unthinkable together, and they had prevailed.

As the base loomed closer, the *Oregon* pressed on, her journey nearly complete. She was scarred but intact, her crew weary but resolute. The mission was behind them, but the lessons they had learned—and the bonds they had forged—would stay with them long after they reached the shore.

Part 2: At the Dock

The *Oregon* cut through the calm waters of the harbor, her once-sleek hull now marred with scars from battle. Scratches ran along her sides like jagged memories, dents from near-misses left her surface uneven, and faint scorch marks traced the edges of where explosions had come far too close. She was a vessel that had survived the impossible, carrying with her not just the weight of her steel but the untold stories of those who had brought her home.

The dock was alive with activity. The technical crew had gathered near the edge, their tools and equipment ready to spring into action. Yet, what caught the crew's attention wasn't the usual flurry of maintenance preparations but the presence of a small, distinguished group standing near the water's edge. High-ranking officers, their pressed uniforms sharp against the muted backdrop of the early morning light, stood waiting. It wasn't protocol. This was something different.

As the *Oregon* slowed to her final approach, a hush seemed to settle over the crew. Green guided the submarine with precision, his hands steady despite the fatigue that weighed on him.

"Helm steady," he announced softly, his voice cutting through the quiet hum of the control room. The tension that had carried them for days was slowly unraveling, replaced by a mix of relief and muted pride.

King stood at the center of the room, his eyes fixed on the dock ahead. He said nothing, but his presence radiated calm authority, a silent acknowledgment of the journey they had completed.

"Ready to secure," Carter said from her station, her voice softer now. "We're home."

When the submarine finally came to a halt and the gangway was lowered, the crew began to emerge. One by one, they climbed onto the deck, the cool air hitting their faces as they stepped into the light of the open sky. Their movements were slow but deliberate, their faces etched with exhaustion. And yet, in their eyes burned a quiet pride—a reflection of the trials they had endured and the mission they had accomplished.

The sight of the submarine was enough to draw murmurs from the gathered officers. The *Oregon* was a battered warrior, her very appearance a testament to the chaos she had braved. As the crew lined up along the deck, standing at attention despite their weariness, the officers approached.

The commanding admiral stepped forward, his sharp eyes scanning the scene before him. He paused, letting the moment stretch as if to absorb the weight of what he was seeing. Then, his gaze fell on King, who had just stepped onto the deck, his uniform still crisp despite the ordeal.

"Captain King," the admiral said, his voice firm but tinged with genuine respect. "You and your crew have accomplished what many would have deemed impossible. Your leadership, and their courage, are a credit to the fleet—and to the nation."

King, ever composed, gave a slight nod. "Thank you, Admiral. It was a team effort. They are the ones who deserve the credit." His voice carried the weight of sincerity, his words directed as much at the crew behind him as the man standing before him.

The admiral's gaze shifted to the crew. "You've brought her back," he said, his voice rising slightly to address them all. "Damaged, yes—but standing. That's a mark of resilience, not just of the vessel, but of the men and women aboard her."

The crew remained at attention, but there was a faint shift among them— a slight straightening of shoulders, a glimmer of pride breaking through the fatigue.

As the officers stepped back, the technical team moved in, inspecting the submarine with careful hands. Landry emerged from the hatch, wiping his hands on a cloth that seemed as worn as he was.

"Captain," he said, stepping to King's side, his tone quieter than usual but filled with satisfaction. "She's held together. Don't ask me how, but she did. We'll patch her up, good as new."

King allowed himself the faintest smile. "She's earned her rest. As have you."

The dock buzzed with activity as the crew began their final descent from the submarine. For a moment, there was no fanfare, no dramatic celebration—just the soft murmur of voices, the clink of tools, and the occasional call of orders. And yet, in that muted scene, there was a heroism that didn't need trumpets or banners.

As King stood on the dock, watching his crew disembark, he felt a quiet sense of closure. The mission was complete, but the journey wasn't just about what they had achieved—it was about what they had become.

The admiral lingered for a moment longer, then approached King once more. "Take care of them," he said simply. "They've earned it."

King nodded, his expression solemn. "They'll be ready for whatever comes next."

As the last of the crew stepped onto solid ground, the *Oregon* sat quietly at the dock, her battle-worn frame a symbol of their perseverance. The mission was over, but the echoes of their journey lingered in the air.

The morning light grew stronger, casting a pale glow over the water and the men and women who had faced the abyss—and returned.

Part 3: The Captain's Report

The quiet hum of the naval base seemed to echo in the still air as Captain King made his way to the commanding officer's office. The narrow corridors felt heavier than usual, the faint scent of oil and seawater lingering like a shadow of the mission they had just completed. His polished boots struck the floor in even steps, but inside, his mind churned with the weight of everything that had transpired.

When he reached the heavy oak door, he paused briefly, taking a steadying breath. The plaque on the door read *Admiral William Carter*, its brass letters gleaming in the muted light. King lifted a hand and knocked, his movements precise yet deliberate.

"Enter," came the voice from within, firm and steady.

King pushed the door open and stepped inside, his posture as straight and composed as ever. The admiral sat behind a broad desk, its surface immaculate except for a single open file and a cup of coffee. He looked up, his sharp eyes studying King with a mixture of curiosity and respect.

"Captain King," the admiral began, gesturing to the chair opposite him. "Take a seat."

King obeyed, lowering himself into the chair with measured precision. The silence stretched for a moment, heavy but not uncomfortable. Then the admiral spoke again.

"I've read the preliminary report, but I want to hear it from you. Start from the beginning."

King's jaw tightened briefly before he nodded. His hands rested lightly on his knees, his gaze focused but distant, as if he were looking through the admiral and into the depths of the ocean they had just left.

"The mission began as planned," he began, his voice steady but carrying a weight that seemed to deepen with each word. "We entered the operational zone undetected and initiated the data-gathering protocols. For the first twenty-four hours, everything proceeded smoothly. But then…"

He paused, the memory of that first sonar ping flashing through his mind—the moment they realized the *Sokol* was closer than expected.

"We encountered unforeseen resistance. The Soviet forces were more aggressive than anticipated. They deployed active sonar, patrol aircraft, and torpedoes in an effort to intercept us."

As he spoke, King recounted each maneuver, each decision, each moment when the *Oregon* teetered on the edge of disaster. He described the near-misses, the damaged systems, and the creative solutions his crew had devised under pressure.

"They were remarkable," he said, his voice softening for the first time. "Every single member of that crew performed beyond expectation. From Green's precise navigation to Carter's tireless monitoring, to Landry keeping the systems running under impossible conditions… They are the reason we made it back."

The admiral nodded slightly, his expression unreadable.

"But," King continued, his tone shifting, "it wasn't without cost."

He leaned forward slightly, his elbows resting on his knees, his fingers lacing together.

"The *Oregon* sustained significant damage. The hull integrity is compromised in several places, and the propulsion systems require extensive repairs. But more than that…" He paused, his voice catching for just a moment. "The crew. They're strong, but they're carrying the weight of what we went through. The stress, the fear—it's something that doesn't just disappear when you dock."

The admiral's expression hardened, not with anger but with understanding. He had seen it before—the toll such missions took on even the best crews.

"You did what had to be done," the admiral said, his voice firm but not unkind. "And you brought them home. That's what matters."

King leaned back slightly, his composure returning.
"I accept full responsibility for the decisions made during the mission. Every risk, every maneuver—they were my calls. But I stand by them. The mission was a success, and that's because of the crew."

The admiral studied him for a long moment, his fingers steepled beneath his chin.
"You're right," he said finally. "It was a success. And it's clear that your leadership was instrumental in that success. But Captain, you know as well as I do that the fleet doesn't just need ships. It needs leaders—leaders like you."

King's jaw tightened again, and for the first time, a flicker of something uncertain crossed his face.

"With respect, sir," he said, his voice low, "the fleet also needs crews that aren't pushed to their breaking point."

The admiral raised an eyebrow, but he didn't argue. Instead, he leaned back in his chair, his gaze sharpening.

"I won't pretend to know what you're feeling," the admiral said. "But I do know this: you've earned the respect of everyone in this room and beyond it. The decision on what comes next is yours, Captain. But whatever you choose, know that you've already done more than most could ever hope to."

King nodded, his expression neutral but his thoughts a storm. As he rose from the chair, he saluted sharply, the motion crisp and precise.

"Thank you, Admiral," he said.

The admiral returned the salute, watching silently as King turned and left the room.

As the door closed behind him, King exhaled slowly, the weight of the mission still heavy on his shoulders. Each step down the corridor felt deliberate, each breath a reminder of the choices he had made and the ones still to come.

He wasn't just leaving a report behind in that room—he was leaving a part of himself.

Part 4: The Decision

The dim light of the captain's quarters cast long shadows across the walls as King sat at his desk, staring at the blank sheet of paper before him. His pen hovered above it, suspended by an invisible weight that seemed to pull him in two directions. The room was silent except for the faint hum of the base outside and the occasional creak of the *Oregon's* settling hull.

He leaned back in his chair, the pen slipping from his fingers onto the desk. His gaze drifted to the far wall, where a neatly framed map of the world hung. Each ocean, each current, each depth was familiar to him, like the lines on his own hands. He had spent most of his life navigating those waters, commanding vessels like the *Oregon*, leading men and women into the unknown. But now, for the first time, the thought of stepping onto the bridge filled him not with resolve, but with weariness.

His thoughts wandered back to his first command, the nervous energy he had carried as a young officer. He remembered the pride, the exhilaration, and the sharp pangs of fear that came with responsibility. Over the years, those emotions had tempered into something steadier, but they had never disappeared entirely. Every decision he had made, every mission he had undertaken, had carved itself into him, leaving marks invisible to the eye but heavy on his soul.

He thought of the *Oregon's* most recent mission—the risks, the near misses, the lives balanced precariously on every order he gave. His crew had performed beyond expectation, but the cost was clear in their weary faces, in the haunted looks that lingered even now.

King exhaled slowly, the sound breaking the silence like a ripple on calm water. He knew what he had to do.

The next morning, King found Green in the control room, reviewing reports with his usual meticulous attention. The younger officer glanced up as the captain approached, straightening reflexively.

"Captain," Green said, his tone professional but warm.

"Walk with me," King replied simply, gesturing toward the corridor.

As they walked through the quiet halls of the submarine, King spoke without preamble.
"You've done exceptional work, Green. Not just on this mission, but in every command I've given you. You've shown composure under pressure, quick thinking, and an ability to lead."

Green's brow furrowed slightly, sensing something deeper beneath the words. "Thank you, sir. I've learned from the best."

King allowed himself a faint smile. "You're ready, Green. Ready for more responsibility. The fleet needs officers like you—ones who can adapt, innovate, and carry us into the future."

They stopped at the hatch leading to the dock, the faint morning light filtering in. Green turned to him, his expression serious. "Are you saying…?"

King nodded, his gaze steady. "I've decided to step down. It's time for me to pass the torch."

Later that day, Carter found King in the officer's mess, where he was nursing a cup of coffee. She approached cautiously, her expression a mixture of curiosity and concern.

"I heard a rumor," she began, sitting down across from him. "Tell me it's not true."

King didn't look up immediately. Instead, he took a slow sip of his coffee, letting the words settle. When he finally met her eyes, his expression was calm but resolute.

"It's true," he said simply.

Carter leaned back in her chair, crossing her arms. "You're serious about this? After everything we've been through?"

King's gaze softened. "That's exactly why I'm serious. I've had my time, Carter. It's been an honor, but it's time for someone else to take the lead. Someone who can see things with fresh eyes."

For a moment, Carter looked as though she might argue, but then her expression shifted. She nodded slowly, the tension in her shoulders easing. "If this is what you believe is right, then I'll trust your judgment. But know this—you've set the bar high. Whoever follows you will have a hell of a legacy to live up to."

That evening, King returned to his quarters and sat once more at his desk. This time, the pen in his hand felt lighter. He began to write, the words flowing easily now.

To the Commanding Admiral,
Effective immediately, I am submitting my resignation as captain of the USS Oregon. It has been the greatest honor of my life to serve in this capacity and to command such an exceptional crew. However, I believe it is time for a new generation of leaders to take the helm—officers who will carry forward the lessons we've learned and the values we hold dear.

He paused, his hand steady, before adding the final words:

With respect and gratitude,
Robert King

As he signed his name, a sense of peace settled over him. It wasn't an ending—it was a transition. One chapter was closing, but another was beginning, for both him and the *Oregon*.

The next morning, as the first rays of sunlight touched the base, King handed the letter to the admiral's aide. He turned to face the dock where the *Oregon* rested, her scars illuminated in the soft light. He stood there for a long moment, taking it all in—the ship, the sea, and the memories he would carry with him.

And then, with a final glance, he walked away, leaving the bridge behind but knowing it was in good hands.

Part 5: Farewell

The metallic hum of the *Oregon*'s systems reverberated softly through the hull, a sound so familiar it felt like the heartbeat of the vessel. The crew had gathered in the control room, their usual positions temporarily abandoned. There was no official ceremony, no pomp or formality—just a group of men and women who had weathered the impossible together, coming to say goodbye to the one who had led them through it all.

King stood near the captain's chair, his hands lightly resting on its back. The room felt both smaller and larger than he remembered—smaller because of the weight of the moment, larger because of the people who filled it. He looked around, meeting each gaze in turn. These weren't just sailors or officers. They were his crew, his family.

When he finally spoke, his voice was steady, but there was a warmth to it that softened the edges.

"I won't keep you long," he began, his eyes sweeping the room. "We've been through more together than most crews ever will. We've faced danger, uncertainty, and moments when the odds seemed insurmountable. And yet, here we are. Not because of one person, but because of all of you."

He paused, letting the words settle, his gaze lingering on each face.

"You're the strongest team I've ever served with," he continued, his tone deepening with sincerity. "Not because you followed orders, but because you trusted each other. That trust—your unity—is what brought us home. And it's what will carry you forward, long after I'm gone."

A ripple of emotion passed through the room. Some stood a little straighter, their expressions hardening with pride. Others shifted, their eyes glistening with unshed tears. Green stood near the navigation console, his jaw tight, his hands clasped behind his back. Carter watched intently from her station, her usual sharp focus softened by the moment. Landry leaned casually against a bulkhead, but even he couldn't hide the flicker of emotion in his usually stoic face.

King straightened slightly, his hands gripping the back of the chair for a moment before releasing it.

"I'm proud of what we've accomplished together," he said, his voice quieter now. "But it's time for me to step aside. This ship—this crew—deserves a leader who can take you to the next chapter. And I have no doubt that leader is already among you."

He turned slightly, gesturing toward Green, who stiffened reflexively under the attention.

"Lieutenant Green," King said, his tone formal but filled with respect, "I've watched you grow into an officer of exceptional skill and character. You have the instincts, the discipline, and the heart to lead. I'm leaving this ship in your hands, knowing it couldn't be in better ones."

Green stepped forward, his movements sharp and precise. "Thank you, Captain," he said, his voice firm but carrying a note of reverence.

King nodded once, then stepped back, his hands brushing against the armrests of the captain's chair one last time. He turned toward the crew once more, his posture straight but his expression soft.

"You've given me more than I could ever repay," he said. "Thank you—for your service, for your trust, and for allowing me the privilege of being your captain."

For a moment, there was silence. Then, almost as one, the crew snapped to attention. The sound of boots striking the floor echoed through the control room as they saluted. The gesture was crisp, disciplined, but beneath it lay a depth of emotion that no regulation could dictate.

King returned the salute, his movements slow, deliberate. He let the moment stretch, committing each face, each detail, to memory.

As the crew broke formation, some approached him. Landry clapped him on the shoulder, murmuring a gruff but heartfelt, "We'll miss you, Captain." Carter lingered for a moment before offering a quiet, "It's been an honor, sir." Even Green allowed himself a rare smile as he shook King's hand firmly.

Finally, the room began to clear, the crew returning to their stations, leaving King alone with Green.

"You'll do well," King said simply, his hand resting briefly on Green's shoulder.

Green nodded, his voice steady. "I'll do my best, Captain."

King took one last look around the control room. Every panel, every console, every corner held memories. His gaze lingered on the captain's chair, now officially Green's, before he turned and walked toward the exit.

The metal floor beneath his boots felt different this time—lighter, somehow. As he ascended the ladder, the hum of the *Oregon* followed him, a familiar sound that felt like a final goodbye.

On the deck, the morning air was cool against his face. The harbor stretched out before him, the base coming alive with activity. He stood there for a moment, looking back at the submarine that had been his home, his responsibility, and his legacy.

With a final nod, he descended the gangway, his steps steady, his heart full. The *Oregon* would sail on without him, but a part of him would always remain aboard.

Part 6: New Horizons

The crisp morning air carried the faint tang of salt as King stood at the edge of the base, his gaze fixed on the *Oregon*. The submarine rested silently in the harbor, her battered hull glinting under the rising sun. Nearby, the technical crews were already swarming over her, assessing damage, logging repairs, and preparing her for the missions yet to come. The sight filled him with a mix of pride and melancholy.

This was the end of a chapter—his chapter.

King's hands rested lightly in the pockets of his uniform, his stance relaxed yet rooted. As he watched the activity around the *Oregon*, he couldn't help but feel the duality of the moment. On one hand, there was relief: relief that the mission was over, that his crew was safe, and that he could finally step back. But alongside that relief was a faint bitterness, a pang of loss at leaving behind the vessel and the people who had become so much a part of him.

A faint hum of machinery reached his ears as he saw Green step out onto the deck of the *Oregon.* The young officer, now captain, moved with the same precision and confidence that King had come to respect. Green was already speaking with one of the technical officers, his gestures clear and commanding, though tinged with the humility of someone stepping into such a monumental role.

King smiled faintly. *He's ready,* he thought.

Nearby, Carter stood on the bridge, her sharp eyes scanning a tablet as she coordinated system diagnostics with the engineering team. Despite her focus, there was a lightness to her movements, a sense of readiness for whatever lay ahead. She glanced toward the dock and saw King watching. For a brief moment, their gazes met, and she gave him a subtle nod—an acknowledgment, a silent promise that she would carry forward what he had instilled in them all.

King returned the nod, a small but meaningful gesture. He didn't need words to convey his pride in her. Carter was a force of nature, someone who had proven herself time and again. She would thrive in this new chapter, just as Green would.

The base bustled with activity around him, but King felt strangely detached, as though he were already stepping into another world. His role here was finished, and the *Oregon,* though still a part of him, was no longer his responsibility. That knowledge brought a strange combination of weight and freedom.

He took one last look at the submarine, her scars now symbols of survival rather than weakness. She had endured—and so had her crew.

As he turned to leave, he was approached by an aide carrying a small bundle wrapped in cloth. The young sailor looked nervous but determined as he extended the package.

"Captain," the sailor said, his voice formal but tinged with respect. "From the crew."

King unwrapped the cloth to reveal a polished brass plaque. It was engraved with the words:
To Captain Robert King—For Guiding Us Through the Depths.

For a moment, King said nothing. He ran his fingers over the engraved letters, feeling the weight of the gift, both literal and symbolic.

"Thank you," he finally said, his voice quiet but firm. The sailor saluted sharply before stepping back, leaving King alone with the plaque.

As he walked away from the harbor, the sound of the *Oregon's* repairs faded into the background. The path ahead was uncertain, but that no longer intimidated him. He had given everything he could to the *Oregon* and her crew, and now it was time for new horizons—for them and for him.

The road stretched out before him, bathed in the soft morning light. With each step, he felt lighter, as though the burdens of command were slowly lifting. Yet within that lightness was a profound sense of fulfillment. He had done his duty. He had made his mark. And though his path was leading him away from the sea, he knew that its echoes would remain with him forever.

In the distance, the *Oregon* stood tall and unyielding, a monument to resilience and unity. Behind him, a new chapter was beginning, filled with fresh challenges and the promise of tomorrow.

And with that, Captain Robert King walked forward, leaving behind a legacy that would sail on in the hearts of those he had led.

Epilogue

The dimly lit cabin of the *Sokol* was a stark contrast to the blinding light of the interrogation chamber just days prior. Captain Vasily Kovalenko sat at his desk, his pen moving steadily across the rough pages of his official report. The hum of the submarine's systems provided a familiar background rhythm, a sound that had accompanied him through countless missions, each one leaving its indelible mark on his soul.

The room smelled faintly of oil and the metallic tang of seawater, a reminder of their prolonged time below the surface. On the desk before him lay a half-empty glass of vodka, its contents untouched since he poured it. It was not a time for indulgence, but for reflection.

Kovalenko paused, lifting his pen from the page as he leaned back in his chair. The memory of the past weeks unfolded in his mind like a chessboard. Each move, each counter-move, played out with precise calculation. The Americans had been clever—relentlessly clever. Their submarine had slipped through his grasp like a shadow in the depths, defying the odds and outmaneuvering his every strategy.

For a moment, frustration bubbled to the surface. He clenched his fist, the creak of leather breaking the silence. But as quickly as it rose, the frustration subsided, replaced by something far more unexpected: respect.

He picked up his pen again and began to write, his words flowing with the rhythm of conviction.

"The American submarine displayed an extraordinary level of skill and discipline. Their captain, whoever he may be, conducted his vessel with the precision of a grandmaster in a high-stakes match. Their evasion tactics were not only resourceful but daring, bordering on the impossible. It was a battle of wits, fought in the unseen depths, and though they eluded us, I cannot deny the mastery they demonstrated."

Kovalenko paused once more, this time to take a sip of water from a steel cup. He glanced toward the small, round porthole on the opposite wall.

Beyond it, the sea stretched endlessly, cold and indifferent. It had been their stage, their arena, and while it bore no memory of their struggle, it had witnessed the unspoken rules of the game.

He continued writing, his pen carving out words that felt heavier than usual.

"Though this engagement did not end in our favor, it is a stark reminder that we are not facing amateurs or cowards. The Americans are formidable opponents, driven by their own sense of duty and resolve. This mission, while a loss strategically, was a testament to the reality of this silent war. Neither side seeks open conflict, yet neither can afford to lose ground. It is a balancing act as precarious as walking a knife's edge."

The hum of the *Sokol* seemed louder in the silence that followed. Kovalenko leaned back once more, his pen resting on the desk, his hand hovering near the glass of vodka. But instead of reaching for it, he let his gaze wander. He thought of his own crew—the tension in their faces, the resolve in their actions. They had done everything he had asked of them, and more.

Just as the Americans had a captain who led them through the abyss, so too did the *Sokol* have its own crew of warriors, silent and unseen, yet unwavering in their purpose.

He wrote his final thoughts, the words etched with a mix of resignation and determination.

"This mission has shown me that while we may win battles, the true war is one of patience and respect. The ocean does not belong to us alone. It is shared by those who are willing to stake their lives for what they believe. While I cannot condone their actions, I cannot help but respect their commitment. This silent war will continue, of that I have no doubt. But as we move forward, let us not underestimate those who challenge us. For in underestimating them, we risk losing ourselves."

As Kovalenko signed his name at the bottom of the report, he allowed himself a rare moment of stillness. The war would not end here—of that he was certain. But he also knew that battles like these, fought in the shadowed depths of the sea, were not just tests of strength. They were tests of humanity, of will, of understanding.

He stood, tucking the report into its envelope and sealing it with care. Turning toward the porthole, he stared out into the endless blue-gray expanse.

"Next time," he murmured softly, his voice carrying both a challenge and a promise.

And with that, Captain Vasily Kovalenko stepped away from his desk, his resolve as unyielding as the steel that encased his vessel.

Thank you for choosing *Silent Depths: A Cold War Submarine Thriller* and diving into the hidden depths of this story. It has been an incredible privilege to share this journey with you—a tale of courage, strategy, and survival beneath the waves. I hope it has brought you moments of tension, excitement, and reflection.

If you found this story engaging, your review can make a tremendous impact. By sharing your thoughts on Amazon, you help other readers discover this book and support authors like me in creating more stories that captivate and inspire.

I would love to hear what resonated with you most—whether it was the high-stakes decisions, the complex characters, or the chilling reality of life in the deep sea. Your feedback is invaluable and deeply appreciated.

Thank you for being part of this adventure, for stepping into the silent depths and exploring the hidden worlds of espionage and survival. Stories like this come alive because of readers like you.

Warm regards,
Art Venka

Printed in Dunstable, United Kingdom